CHATSWOOD CATHOLIC CEMETERY

C. 1865 – C. 1911

Joan Newman Antarakis

Red Raven Books

RED RAVEN BOOKS
Publisher: The Copy Collective PL, 7 Blackfriars St, Chippendale NSW, 2008
Copyright © 2014 Joan Newman Antarakis

All rights reserved. No part of this publication may be reproduced, distributed or transmitted in any form or by any means, stored in or introduced to a retrieval system, or transmitted in any form of by any means (electronic, mechanical, photocopying, recording or otherwise), without the prior consent of the author and the publisher of the book

National Library of Australia Cataloguing-in-Publication Data. A catalogue record for this book is available on request from the National Library of Australia

Book Layout ©2013 BookDesignTemplates.com
Printed and bound by Ingram Book Group, Inc.
ISBN 978-1-925154-02-3

Preface

The following list of burials in the Chatswood Catholic Cemetery has taken several years to research and prepare for publication. Numerous people have been supportive and extremely patient. After finishing the Chatswood Parish history in 2001, it was my intention to complete work on the cemetery in time for the parish centenary in 2010. Owing to the small number of known burials, 57 and the dozen or so I later discovered, this task did not at first appear too difficult. My aim was to provide short biographies of those 57 plus the additional 12. But curiosity prevailed and I went in search of more burial details with the aim of reaching 100 and like Topsy it 'just growed'. And once again when the publishers were ready to begin work yet another group of burials was found. While a supplementary list has been added, it has not been possible to conduct extensive research beyond confirming this is indeed correct. The final total is now 169.

Over many years, the deceased and their stories have captured my interest especially when I discovered that several of those buried at Chatswood were convicts while members of their families and siblings were either convicts or married to convicts. There may be other convicts buried here but as yet I have not been able to establish this with certainty. There emerged evidence of close ties to the First, Second and Third Fleets as well as the early military regiments. Research of the families, their work, friendships and in some cases disputes, convinced me that despite what appeared to be a sparsely settled area prior to the construction of railway lines, the people of the North Shore knew and interacted with their neighbours. My hope is that this work will now provide a lasting memorial to the many extraordinary settlers and pioneers who came early: c. 1830 - 1910- to this beautiful area on Sydney's North Shore.

Introduction

The Catholic Cemetery in Anderson Street, Chatswood, on Sydney's North Shore, was closed to burials in 1917 by order of the Council. A large portion was redeveloped in the late 1940s. To the hundreds of residents and visitors who pass by each day there is no visible evidence that a cemetery ever occupied the site. A portion of St. Pius X College is situated on the old burial ground and in its Monastery chapel there is a memorial plaque with the names of 57 persons who were buried there. No extant burial records, apart from this list, are available. The 57 names were inscribed on headstones removed from the site when the cemetery was cleared to provide space for additional school buildings. Former students have memories of headstones being stored under temporary classrooms during the 1950s. Parish archival records indicate that Reverend Father (Rev. Fr.) William O'Flynn, Parish Priest (P.P.) sought permission from the Archdiocese to use the disused cemetery land for school buildings in 1948.

Later, in 1985, when extensions to the College were under construction, several broken headstones were exposed. These were taken away for preservation and for many years were stored at Willoughby City Library. Extensive research has enabled the compiler to contribute additional names bringing the total of known burials to 169, of these 11 names are on a Supplementary List and 30 foundlings from the Waitara Foundling Home on the North Shore are listed separately. It is hoped that evidence of many more burials will be found.

Details on Death Certificates indicate several name changes occurred to the cemetery after 1864, including:

1. *North Shore Catholic Burial Ground* - 1865
2. *Roman Catholic St. Leonards* -1869
3. *Lane Cove R.C. Cemetery/Burial Ground* 1871-1893
4. *North Willoughby Catholic Cemetery c. 1876-1882*
5. *Cooper's Flat, Catholic Cemetery, Chatswood. c. 1899-1911*

A Willoughby resident named Cooper had a hut in the immediate vicinity. There are entries for three families named Cooper in Willoughby records.

(1) William Cooper, a native of Surrey, England and his family lived close by in Mowbray Road, Willoughby in 1891 about the time the cemetery had a change of name. A child, Esther May Cooper was born to William and Martha Emily Norman on 27 June 1891 at Mowbray Road, North Willoughby.[1]

(2) A funeral notice of 18 February 1907 stated that Esther Cooper, late of Willoughby Road was buried at Gore Hill. In 1871, the *Sands Directory* listed a Mrs Cooper living at Fitzroy Street and Lane Cove Road, St. Leonards.

(3) A Francis Cooper appears in North Willoughby Rate Books as owning 21 acres (8.4984 ha) of bush land at Lane Cove.

The earliest recorded cemetery on the North Shore was on land Alexander Berry donated to St. Thomas' Anglican Church for a burial ground at St. Leonards and the first recorded burial there was in 1845. This cemetery was sometimes referred to as *The Willoughby Cemetery* as well as *St. Leonards Cemetery*. A second Anglican Cemetery, St. John's, was opened in 1867 at Gordon on the Upper North Shore.

The Methodist church (now Uniting Church) established a cemetery at the corner of Lane Cove Road (Pacific Highway) and Mowbray Road (South Chatswood) in 1871.

Prior to 1863 Catholics living on the north side of Sydney Harbour experienced great difficulties when faced with the task of interring deceased family members. Their options were a burial ground located in the centre of Sydney at Devonshire Street (later Central Railway) or further away at Haslem's Creek, (Rookwood). To access these cemeteries it was necessary to cross the harbour by horse punt or ferry. Mourners travelling to the cemetery at St Charles Ryde, established c. 1850, went by special steamer.

William Tunks, Member Legislative Assembly (MLA) and first Mayor of St. Leonards, is credited with securing land for Gore Hill General Cemetery in 1867. In a letter dated March 1867 he stated "... to convey the dead from the Parishes of Willoughby and Gordon to Haslem's Creek for burial will be inconvenient and even oppressive to many poor families ..."[2] Gore Hill Cemetery was dedicated in 1868 and finally closed in 1974. However burials did not take place immediately. In the Catholic portion, the first recorded burial took place on 2 February 1877.

William Lithgow was Attorney General from 1824. Lithgow subdivided land on the north side of Sydney Harbour with an area of approximately 600 acres (243 ha). In 1854, he named the subdivision *The Township of North Sydney*. The land acquired by Lithgow was originally granted to Richard Archbold by Sir Thomas Brisbane, in 1825. After Archbold's death around 1836 the grant was withdrawn. The land was later granted to John Stirling, chairman of the Joint Stock Banking Company, aka *Bank of Australia,* by Sir Charles Augustus Fitzroy in 1850. The remains of Richard Archbold were reinterred in Chatswood Cemetery in 1901 following the clearance of Devonshire Street Cemetery to make way for Central Railway Station. Today Chatswood takes in that original area and a great deal more. By the 1860s, it was acknowledged that there was an urgent need for burial grounds on the North Shore. Catholic burials required long and difficult journeys by mourners, in all weathers, down through the dense bushland to the Harbour shore and then ferried across to the southern shore. All these events took place long before the construction of railways on the North Shore and decades before the construction of Sydney Harbour Bridge. Following the building of railway lines on the North Shore in the 1890s, access to cemeteries became easier.

Three parcels of land were set aside in the Archer and Anderson Street area, by William Lithgow, for burial grounds for the Presbyterian, Anglican and Catholic churches. These portions were all adjoining and known as the Grafton Plains Estate. The Catholics immediately used their land for burials. The Anglicans built a church, some distance away, on Mowbray Road, and again later, in 1902 a second church on Fuller's Road, Chatswood. The Lithgow grant to the Anglican church was subdivided and sold off as the Chatswood Park Estate. The Presbyterian church retained most of its grant until 1912, when a portion was sold off as the Kirk Estate.

The portion, allocated for Catholic burials, was granted by a Deed of Gift for 3 acres, 1 rood and 24 perches (2.8 ha), dated 7 September 1863 signed by William Lithgow of St. Leonards, Rev. Peter Powell, Catholic pastor; John Sylvester Ryan Esquire (Esq.), and Thomas Cosgrove, a baker.[3] J. S. Ryan owned land in present day Naremburn and was Auditor for the borough of North Willoughby in 1870. Thomas Cosgrove, from County Cavan, Ireland was later buried in the cemetery in 1871.The minister who conducted the funeral service was Rev. John Kenny, second parish priest of the North Shore. Rev. Peter Powell was the first parish priest on the North Shore and was a contemporary of Rev. Fr. Therry. He was described as 6ft tall (180cms) and a splendid horseman. He visited Mt. Gambier, South Australia where he joined Fr. Julian Tenison Woods who later, in 1866, met and befriended Mary McKillop. Mary McKillop was declared a Saint in 2010. Fr. Powell settled finally at St. Leonards, Sydney, where he became parish priest in 1856. He resigned in March 1867 and left for England on the *Jason* and died in Belgium five years later.[4]

Claude Leplastrier, a Willoughby Council alderman, wrote in his local history that by 1917 Willoughby Council had passed a by-law prohibiting burials in the municipality within 50 feet (15.2m) of the road. The last known burial, in what was then Cooper's Flat Catholic cemetery, took place in 1911. But Lepastrier puts the last burial date as occurring just prior to WW1 (1914).[5] By 1911 Willoughby Municipality covered an area of approximately 9 sq. miles (23.31 sq.

kilometres), and included Naremburn and part of St. Leonards. The population numbered 10,000 occupying 2,635 dwellings.

In the absence of burial records or headstones (apart from the 1985 list of 57 names) every effort has been employed to ensure this list is correct. Records of the State and Mitchell Libraries, New South Wales (NSW) State Records and collections of historical and genealogical societies have been searched. Certificates and Birth, Deaths and Marriages, (BDM) transcripts were also purchased, newspapers searched, descendants contacted when possible and lists of North Shore cemeteries checked.

There were additional difficulties as the cemetery had several name changes while the area in and around Chatswood experienced name change as well. William Lithgow named his land, the township of North Sydney (present day Chatswood). Earlier, in 1805, Isaac Nichols received a grant of 200 acres (80 ha) in the district of Hunter's Hill and called it King's Plains. Today it is the site of Chatswood Railway Station and surrounds. Earlier, Chatswood could be referred to as North Willoughby. And registration details, in particular registrations of death, were often inaccurate or incomplete. The area on the north side of Sydney Harbour was called Hunter's Hill in the 1828 Census and appeared on Land Grants as early as the mid 1790s. The area on the lower North Shore of Sydney Harbour, at St. Leonards, changed to North Sydney with St. Leonards now describing an area further north. The name Lane Cove identified the country all the way up to and beyond present day Pymble as early as 1788. Up until the 20th century many deaths on the North Shore were registered at St. Leonards. So the name and location of the cemetery was often unclear and the religion of the deceased person might be omitted from the death certificate. And in those early years, there might be no minister of religion present at the burial and members of the immediate family, or friends, acted as undertaker. Owing to the very small number of burials as yet confirmed, some biographical material is included as well as relevant local history. Additional information came from descendants of early pioneers and other generous people interested in recording and preserving North Shore history.

List of Burials

1. **ALFONSO**, Percival Augustine
Born: 1879, St. Leonards, NSW
Died: 23 December 1879, Myrtle Street, St. Leonards[6]
Age: 4 ½ months
C.O.D.: Catarrhal pneumonia
Buried: 24 December 1879, Catholic Cemetery Lane Cove
Father: Denis/Dionisio Alfonso, builder and carpenter
Mother: Mary Stronach, born 1830, Spain, married 1859, Sydney
Siblings: Mary I., Herbert D., Arthur J., Alfred E., Edith E., Clara M.
Remarks: Denis Alfonso, born Saragossa Spain, died 1899 and buried in Gore
Hill Cemetery.[7]

2. **ARCHBOLD**, Richard Charlemont/Charles
Born: c. 1793, Eadestown, County Kildare, Ireland
Died: 22 October 1836, *Clanville,* Roseville, NSW
Age: abt. 41 years
C.O.D.: unknown

Buried: Devonshire Street Cemetery and reinterred at Chatswood during clearance to make way for Central Railway
Father: Richard Latin Archbold
Mother: Mary Caulfield
Spouse: Mary Clement Pawley, married in Colony of NSW 1817
Children: Eliza 1818, Mary 1821, Richard Charles II 1823, Sarah 1824, Elizabeth 1828, Gerald 1829, Sarah 1831, James (Jacob) 1834, Geraldine 1836
Remarks: Convicted Dublin, Ireland August 1813, sentenced to transportation for seven
years. Sailed from Falmouth, 8 December 1813, on 495 ton *Three Bees* and arrived on 6 May 1814, a voyage of 149 days. Married in 1817 to Mary Clement Pawley, 15-year-old daughter of John Pawley and Hannah. The Pawleys were early convict settlers. John was tried at the Old Bailey and sentenced to seven years and transportation. He arrived on *Admiral Barrington* in October 1791 with the Third Fleet. His occupation, a Tailor.[8]
Hannah Murphy née Von Depthenberg was born c. 1767 in Brussells and arrived in the colony as a convict on the *Mary Ann* in 1791. Her sentence also seven years. Hannah was free by servitude in 1811.[9] John and Mary married in 1794. An advertisement in the *Sydney Gazette* in 1819 places Richard Archbold at the Rocks, Sydney operating a school.[10] By 1822, as listed in the *General Muster,* Archbold was Licensed Victualler at Sydney with Mary his wife, children, Eliza and Mary. These three were born in the colony.[11] In 1825 James Dawson was charged with stealing two casks the property of Richard Archbold and was sentenced to three years at Port Macquarie. The 1828 Census records Richard as aged 35, and free by servitude, a landholder at Hunter's Hill with five children. His wife Mary was 26 years of age, Eliza nine years, Mary seven, Richard

five, Sarah three, and a one-year-old infant.[12] Archbold was granted 600 acres (242 ha) at Roseville, NSW on Sydney's North Shore, finally settling on land he named *Clanville Estate*. Children married into the Servais, Clarke, Wilson, McIntosh, Oliver, Bainbrigge families. Captain Thomas Bainbrigge was Comptroller of Excise with the 57th Regt.[13] His name on extant headstone uncovered in 1985 by Christian Brothers, Chatswood.[14]

3. ARCHBOLD, Richard Charles II

Born: 3 August 1823, Sydney NSW

Died: 3 August 1902, at *Clanville*, Roseville, Sydney.[15]

Age: 79 years, orchardist

C.O.D.: unknown

Father: Richard C. Archbold I

Mother: Mary C. Pawley

Spouse: Mary Isabella Wilson, married 22 July 1851, Church of England (C of E) Willoughby.[16]

Mary Isabella was daughter of G. Wilson of Lane Cove and niece of late Robert Mackintosh Esq.

Children: Sara born 1852, Mary Theresa born 1854, Richard Charles born 1856, James George born 1858, Sydney Patrick born 1860, Elizabeth Australia born 1862, Frances Geraldine born 1864, Florence Emily born 1868, Mabel Constance born 1870, Albert Edward born 1873.

4. ARCHBOLD, Sarah

Born: c. 1824, Sydney, NSW

Died: 8 September 1847[17]

Age: 23 years

C.O.D.: unknown

Buried: at Devonshire Street, and reinterred at Chatswood
Father: Richard Charlemont Archbold. Sarah was his third daughter
Mother: Mary C. Pawley. Mary Archbold died in August 1850. She was 48 years.
Sarah's name on a headstone uncovered in 1985 by Christian Brothers, Chatswood

5. **BALSAM/BALSOM/BALSOMOS née Ryan, Catherine**
Born: c. 1832, Thurles, County Tipperary, Ireland.
Died: 5 July 1900, Pitt Water Road, St. Ives, NSW[18]
Age: 68 years
C.O.D.: Cancer Uterus, Exhaustion
Father: unknown Ryan
Mother: unknown
Spouse: (1) William Christopher Smith, married age 22 years – not found. (2) Louis Balsom, gold miner, married 1876, Bathurst, NSW[19]
Children: 1st Marriage: Smith: Alfred born 1855, Mary A. (Hodges) 44, Emily I (Gallen) 36, Margaret Minerva (Hibberd), 34, Matilda J. (Buhl) 32, William H. 29
Note: Alfred and John Charles deceased by 1900. Elizabeth Margaret born 1860 -
not named on mother's death certificate
Claimed no Issue 2nd Marriage
Marriages of children: Mary Ann Smith, married Albert Hodges, Bathurst, 15 September 1877.[20] Albert Hodges, born Peel, son of John Hodges and Ann Linea, of Glanmire, NSW. Children: Charles, Alfred, Alice, Reginald, Walter O., Emily T. and William G., Mary F., Albert J., Minnie B. and Mildred K. Matilda Josephine Smith

married John Christopher Buhl, Sydney, 22 October 1885.[21] Emily Smith married John Gallen, Sydney, 1884, born Shellharbour[22]
Remarks: Second husband, Louis Balsam/Balsamos born Sicily, Italy c. 1827, died aged 65 years in 1891.[23] He was buried at Wattle Flat Cemetery.[24] Louis was mining for gold on Napoleon Reef at Roxburgh in 1865. He received Certificate of Naturalisation 22 March 1877.[25] An Abel Seaman, he arrived in 1855 on the *Isis*.

6. **BEER, Richard**
Born: c. 1855, Baptism 1855, Sydney [26]
Died: 16 February 1876 at *Woodbridge Farm* [27]
Age: abt. 21 years
C.O.D.: Heart disease
Buried: 19 February 1876 North Willoughby Roman Catholic (R.C.) Cemetery
Father: William Beer, a farmer
Mother: Anna Hannah McDonald
Brothers/sisters: William Beer, Ellen O., Amos D., Ross D.
Witnesses: F.W. Robinson, Ross Beer,
Remarks: William Beer (father) born c. 1827 England and wife Hannah arrived in Sydney, via Melbourne on 23 February 1855 as unassisted passengers.[28]
His name is on the list of 57 burials compiled by Christian Brothers, Chatswood.

7. **BERECRY, Margaret**
Born: c. 1866, Ireland
Died: 13 April 1880, St. Vincent's Hospital, Sydney[29]
Age: 22 years
C.O.D.: Hip disease, Hectic fever

Father: Patrick Berecry
Mother: Mary Ryan
Spouse: not married
Witnesses: Matthew Berecry, John Berecry
Remarks: Time in colony 16 years.

8.   BERECKY/BERECRY, Patrick

Born: Nenagh, County Tipperary, Ireland c. 1821
Died: 13 October 1869, The Infirmary, Sydney[30]
Age: 48 years, labourer
C.O.D.: Peritonitis and liver failure
Buried: 14 October 1869, North Shore R. C. Cemetery
Occupation: labourer
Father: Bryan Berecry
Mother: Margaret unknown
Spouse: Mary Ryan, (daughter of Matthew and Winifred) married County Tipperary.
Mary Berecry died in 1915 at North Sydney and is buried at Gore Hill Cemetery.
Children: Bryan 8, Patrick 6, Winifred 4, Margaret 3, Matthew, an infant
Remarks: Arrived on *Spitfire* 24 August 1863, as Patrick Burcrey.[31] Death registered as Vercry. Son Patrick married Louisa Harris, Bryan Bercry married Maria Maraspen, Winifred married Richard Peters, Margaret married William J. Hudson, Matthew married Anne Mackone. His name is on the list of 57 burials compiled by Christian Brothers, Chatswood.

9.   BORIG, Mary Catherine née Moletor
Born: c. 1821, Germany

Died: 5 January 1875, at Burns Bay, North Sydney[32]
Age: 51 or 54 years
C.O.D.: unknown
Buried: Chatswood R.C. Cemetery
Father: Peter Moletor
Mother: Maria unknown
Spouse: Henrich/Henry Borig, vinedresser, from Kirdorf, Germany
Henry Borig, Senior died in 1907 and was buried in Gore Hill Cemetery
Children: as per shipping lists in 1855, Anna Maria 11, Henrietta 9, Adolph 7, Johan George 4, (Reel 2469 SRA)
Marriages of children: Henry A. married Mary Peddelsden, Johan George married Mary Ann Marsh
Remarks: Arrived in colony per *Cateaux Wattel,* 9 March 1855 from Antwerp.[33]
Maria's brother Peter Moletor was living in Sydney.

10. **BOURKE/BURKE,** Catherine (Kate)
Born: c. 1874, Bobbin Head Road, Lane Cove
Died: 4 August, 1876 [34]
Age: 1 year 10 months
Buried: Chatswood, R.C. Cemetery
Father: Michael J. Bourke. He died in 1901[35]
Mother: Sarah Ann Elizabeth Porter, born Pennant Hills, Sydney
Remarks: Michael J. Bourke arrived in colony, March 1859 per *Hornet* from Clooney, County Sligo, Ireland.[36] His parents were Patrick and Anne. Michael was gardener to the Honourable Richard Hill, at Lane Cove in 1861. He was a fruit grower on six acres (2 ha) fronting Bobbin Road (sic) and Kuringai (sic) Avenue, Turramurra, North Shore. Michael was on the board of the R.C. Denominational

Schools in 1878, He married Sarah Ann Elizabeth Porter, 21 November 1863, at Lane Cove Catholic Church.[37] Sarah was the daughter of Richard Porter of Pennant Hills and Ellen Fitzgerald, Turramurra, NSW.

11. BOURKE/BURKE, Bridget

Born: c. 1872, Sydney[38]
Died: 10 November 1885[39]
Age: 13 years
C.O.D.: unknown
Buried: Chatswood R.C. Cemetery
Father: Michael J. Bourke, 1883 gardener
Mother: Sarah A. Porter

Her name is on the list of 57 recorded burials.

12. BOURKE/BURKE, Ellen Kate

Born: c. 1873
Died: 11 June 1874[40]
Age: 9 months
Buried: Chatswood R.C. Cemetery
Father: Michael J. Bourke
Mother: Sarah A. E. Porter

Her name is on the 1985 list compiled by Christian Brothers, Chatswood.

13. BOYLE, Annie Mary

Born: c. 1853, baptism[41]
Died: 1 October 1877
Age: 24 years
Buried: North Willoughby Catholic Cemetery

Father: Owen Boyle
Mother: Catherine O'Brien[42]
Her name is on the early list of 57 recorded burials.

14. BOYLE, Bridget

Born: c. 1865
Died: 1867[43]
Age: abt. 2 years
C.O.D.: Bronchitis and whooping cough after measles
Buried: 18 April 1867, North Willoughby Catholic Cemetery
Father: Owen Boyle
Mother: Catherine O'Brien
Remarks: Eugene/Owen Boyle acted as undertaker as per death certificate
Witnesses: William Purnell and John Sinour.
Remarks: Eugene Boyle listed as undertaker and no priest in attendance

15. BOYLE, Catherine

Born: c. 1830, Jonestown, County Clare, Ireland
Died: 25 March 1872[44]
Age: abt. 39 years
Buried: Chatswood R.C. Cemetery
Father: Thomas O'Brien
Mother: Catherine unknown
Spouse: Owen Boyle, (aka Eugene) married 25 May 1852, Goulburn NSW[45]
Children; Annie M. born 1854, James born 1857, Joseph born 1862, Bridget born 1865, John T. born 1869

Remarks: Arrived in colony, 12 January per *Panama*. Married Church of Saints Peter and Paul, Goulburn, NSW. Catherine's funeral moved from residence of Mr McCloskey, Hunter Street, Sydney, (SMH). Joseph Owen Boyle, (son) married Emily Thrussell, 1886.[46]

Her name is on the early list of 57 recorded burials.

16. **BOYLE**, Owen aka Eugene
Born: c. 1826, County Fermanagh, Ireland
Died: 12 February 1891[47]
Age: 65 years
C.O.D.: unknown
Buried: Lane Cove Catholic Cemetery
Father: James Boyle
Mother: Ann unknown
Spouse: Catherine O'Brien, married 1852
Remarks: Owen Boyle was landlord of the *Australian Hotel,* Auburn Street, Goulburn in 1853. He was prosecuted for ... selling spirituous and fermented liquors ... to persons in a state of intoxication...[48] In August of 1853, several articles about the hapless Boyle were reported in the *Goulburn Herald* newspaper. In May 1856 the Commercial Banking Company applied to the Supreme Court of New South Wales to sell his stock-in-trade. Trouble again befell Boyle later in 1856 when he was fined twenty shillings for [49] ... letting his pigs stray about on the streets ... And in June the first meeting of his insolvency case was held.[50] In June 1856, Boyle was charged once again for ... suffering a pig to go astray within the town... In March 1860 Owen Boyle was turnkey at Goulburn Gaol and still allowing his pigs to stray. At this time the family resided in Sloane Street, Goulburn. His final clash with the law possibly

convinced him to move his family to Sydney. When Rev. Father Roche visited Goulburn with Archbishop Polding in June 1861 he visited the gaol to perform divine service. While there he gave his coat to the turnkey (Boyle) for safe keeping. On leaving the gaol Rev. Roche discovered that a sum of money was missing. A search of the gaol located the money in the prison yard. Boyle was exonerated and suspicion fell on the prisoner, Hall.[51] By 1865 when Bridget their daughter was born, the birth was registered at St. Leonards, Sydney. John Boyle, a brother, was a signatory on the 1865 Willoughby Petition. Licence issued 26 April 1853 for Australian Hotel, Goulburn, NSW.[52] Owen Boyle and his brother John arrived on the *Pearl* 17 August, 1841.[53]

His name is on the list of 57 recorded burials.

17. **BOYLE, Philip**

Born: c. 1808, County Donegal, Ireland
Died: 27 July 1873 at Lane Cove NSW[54]
Age: abt. 65 years, farmer
C.O.D.: Natural causes
Buried: 29 July 1873, Lane Cove Catholic Cemetery
Father: Denis Boyle
Mother: unknown
Spouse: Ann Senior, born Ann Kelly, County Galway, Ireland c. 1830, married Philip Boyle, 29 July 1870, Star of the Sea, Catholic Church, North Shore[55]
Ann Senior was a widow, 40 years of age. Her father John Kelly and mother Margaret. Ann married David Senior born Yorkshire, England, in Sydney c. 1850
Witnesses: Thomas Senior and John Senior. Owen McMahon was undertaker and no minister of religion present

Remarks: Philip Boyle, a convict, arrived in the colony per *James Laing* 29 June 1834.[56]

He was convicted of picking pockets and sentenced to seven years and transportation. He was 19 years of age. A catholic, no education and occupation, a dealer. Ticket of Leave (TOL) granted 20 November 1838.[57] An Inquest was held into his death at the residence of Owen McMahon at Lane Cove. Ellen McMahon of Allendale Farm, Lane Cove, in evidence stated that Philip Boyle had been an assigned servant of hers. He had previously owned a farm of eight and a half acres (3 ha) which he had sold to Mr John Sainty. He was then lodging at her property and paying ten shillings per week. Boyle had recently complained of shortness of breath and Doctor Ward had attended him. Thomas Senior corroborated this evidence and the jury returned a verdict of ... death from natural causes ...[58]

18. **BRODIE, Margaret**
Born: c. 1826, County Tyrone, Ireland.
Died: 16 February 1865 (earliest known burial in cemetery)[59]
Age: abt. 39 years
Buried: 18 February 1865
Father: William Kenn/Kinnear
Mother: Ellen unknown
Spouse: John Brodie, married Sydney 1856. Brodie was born Fifeshire, Scotland and arrived in 1852 from New York. He established an orchard at Lane Cove
Children: Mary E. born 1860, married Peter Gilroy, August, 1879.[60] Gilroy came from County Sligo, Ireland. He was son of Martin Gilroy and Mary Finnigan
Remarks: Margaret Kinnear, arrived on the *Ebba Brahe* in 1855, from County Tyrone, Ireland. John Brodie (widower) married Ellen

Porter, 30 November 1865.[61] John was on the Denominational School Board in 1878.

19. **BROPHY**, Edward

Born: c. 1822, Queens County, Ireland.
Died: 11 November 1871, Union Street, St. Leonards, NSW[62]
Age: abt. 80 years
Buried: Chatswood Catholic Cemetery
Father: William Brophy
Mother: unknown
Spouse: Margaret Black, born County Tyrone, Ireland, c. 1811, father Robert Black.
Children: A son Henry, baptised 1837[63]
Remarks: Edward Brophy arrived per *Royal Admiral (5)*, 22 January 1835. Tried March 1834 and sentenced to seven years transportation for house breaking.[64] Granted Ticket of Leave in 1842 and allowed to remain in the district of Pitt Water in the service of D. Miller.[65] Sought 'Permission to Marry' Margaret Black (age 34) who arrived free. They married in 1847. Brophy was the first recorded blacksmith in North Sydney and worked from a bark hut in Mount Street. In April 1871 Brophy was evicted and his premises were demolished to make way for the Lane Cove Road. The smithy and butchery were then near Union Street, North Sydney. Jeremiah Crowley, first recorded schoolmaster c. 1860 was Executor of his Will. Margaret Brophy died 12 March 1886 and was buried in Church of England Cemetery, Willoughby. Margaret's nephew W. J. Scott of Lane Cove Road registered her death.[66]
His name is on the list of 57 recorded burials.

20. BURKE, Catherine
Born: c. 1871/72
Died: February 1873[67]
Age: 1 year 1 month
Buried: 15 February 1873, Lane Cove Catholic Cemetery
Father: William Burke
Mother: Sarah Conquit/Corncrake/Cornthwaite

21. BURKE, Sarah Ann
Born: c. 1827 Parramatta NSW
Died: 15 August 1895, at Turramurra, NSW[68]
Age: abt. 68 years
C.O.D.: Broncho Pneumonia
Buried: 17 August 1895, Cooper's Flat, Catholic Cemetery
Father: Thomas Conquit/Corncrake/Cornthwaite. A sawyer
Mother: Frances Martin
Spouse: William Burke, married Parramatta, NSW, 25 October 1846
Children: James 49, John H. 46, Patrick Oliver 42, William 39, Andrew 37, Sarah Jane (Cocks) 35, Thomas 33, Alfred Joseph 26, Peter Clifton 24, 2 males, 1 female (Frances Parfitt) deceased
Remarks: Sarah Ann was a daughter of Thomas Corncrake who arrived in 1819 on board the convict ship *Baring 2*, as Thomas Cornthwaite. Thomas son of Christopher, was born in 1798. Thomas was convicted at Lancaster Quarter Sessions, 19 January 1818 and sentenced to seven years transportation. He was 20 years of age and a sailor. He married Frances Martin at Parramatta in 1835 as Corncrake. Frances was the daughter of John Martin and Mary Randall. John Martin was born in the West Indies c. 1755. He was convicted at the Old Bailey for stealing clothing and sentenced to transportation for seven years. He arrived per the First Fleet convict

ship, *Alexander*.[69] Mary Randall's father, John Randall aka Reynolds, an African/American from Connecticut, USA, also mustered on the First Fleet ship *Alexander* 6 January 1787. He prospered and eventually enlisted in the NSW Corps after selling his 60 acre (24 ha) farm at the Northern Boundary and served from 1800 to 1810. John Randall married Mary Butler a convict, who arrived per the Second Fleet *Neptune* in 1790.[70] His death has not been traced.

22. BURKE, Walter
Born: c. 1867
Died: July 1879[71]
Age: 12 years
Buried: 20 July 1879, North Willoughby Catholic Cemetery
Father: William Burke
Mother: Sarah Conquit/Corncrake/Cornthwaite
Witnesses: William Foster, Hezekiah Gregory.

23. BURKE, William
Born: c. 1814, Dublin, Ireland
Died: 1 December 1890, at Gordon, NSW[72]
Age: abt. 76 years, farmer
C.O.D.: Old age – no medical certificate, inquest dispensed with by Coroner's Order
Buried: Cooper's Flat Cemetery, Chatswood
Father: James Burke, a soldier
Mother: Catherine unknown
Spouse: Sarah Corncrake/Conquit married 1846 at St. Patrick's Church, Parramatta, NSW[73]
Children: Frances born 1851, married John Parfitt in 1874 and died 1891 (see under Parfitt). A. Burke son of deceased registered death

Witnesses: Oliver Burke, Alfred Burke
Remarks: William lived 62 years in the colony

24. CALLAN/CALLEN, Ann Mathew

Born: c. 1830 County Tipperary, Ireland
Died: 29 July 1898, Berry Street, North Sydney[74]
Age: abt. 68 years
C.O.D.: Chronic bronchitis, general dropsy
Buried: 30 July 1898, Cooper's Flat Cemetery Chatswood
Father: unknown Mathew, a saddler
Mother: Ann Naven
Spouse: John Callen, a baker, born County Armagh, Ireland, married St. Mary's Sydney 9 October 1847[75]
Children: George R. born 1858, died 1858; Hannah M. (Lyons) 38, Honora J. (McEwen) 36, James 34, Theobold J.B. 1862. George R. died 11 December 1858, Yurong & Frances Streets, Sydney, aged seven months. By 1862, 5 male children were deceased
Witnesses: Edmond Lyons, James Callen, son of 55 Berry Street, North Sydney
Remarks: Lived about 51 years in New South Wales. Arrived in 1841 per *Fairlie,* with four sisters[76]

25. CALLEN, John

Born: County Armagh, Ireland, c. 1818
Died: 11 August 1899, Berry Street, North Sydney[77]
Age: 81 years, a baker
C.O.D.: Senile decay
Buried: 13 August 1899, Roman Catholic Cemetery, Chatswood
Father: unknown Callen, a farmer
Mother: Jane McCloskey

Spouse: Anne Matthew, married Sydney, NSW
Children: Anna M (Lyons) 43, Honora J. (McEwan) 37, James 35
Witnesses: Luke McDonnell, Leslie Small
Remarks: about one year in Victoria and 57 years in NSW. Arrived on Convict ship *Waverley*, 17 June 1839. Tried Kilkenny, Ireland. Transported for seven years. His occupation, baker.[78]

26. CHERRY, Ann

Born: c. 1816, County Clare, Ireland
Died: 29 September 1879 at Lane Cove[79]
Age: 64 years
Buried: Chatswood Catholic Cemetery
Father: unknown Considine, a farmer
Mother: unknown
Spouse: James Cherry, married c. 1848, County Clare, Ireland
Children: None listed
Remarks: Lived about 30 years in NSW
Her name is on the list of 57 burials recorded by Christian Brothers, Chatswood.[80]

27. CHERRY, John/James

Born: c. 1818, County Clare, Ireland
Died: 2 March 1881[81]
Age: abt. 63 years, fruit grower/orchardist
C.O.D.: Fatty degeneration of the heart (Coroner's finding)
Father: Michael Cherry
Mother: Mary Kane/Cain
Spouse: (1) Ann Considine, married County Clare, Ireland, c. 1845.
(2) Mary Anne Marsh, married 15 May 1880, Sacred Heart Church,

Sydney, /00674.[82] Mary Anne the daughter of Patrick Marsh and Mary Flynn

Children: none listed

Remarks: Lived on 5 acres (2 ha) at Lane Cove (Gordon). Cherry Street in Gordon is named after him. James and wife Ann arrived aboard the *Talavera* in 1853. His brother, Thomas Cherry, and sister, Bridget McInerney were also living in Sydney. James was an associate of Mary and Lawrence Howard. Henry William Dickson of Gordon was executor of his estate, probate value 1253 pounds.[83] An inquest was held at the Gardener's Arms Hotel, North Shore, to enquire into his sudden death. Coroner's finding ... fatty degeneration of the heart.[84]

28. CHUTER, Catherine

Born: c. 1811, Ireland
Died: 6 August 1871, Susannah Street, St. Leonards, NSW[85]
Age: abt. 60 years
Buried: 8 August 1871, Lane Cove Catholic Burial Ground
Father: believed to be John or Mathew Maley, a gardener
Mother: Mary Ryan
Spouse: (1) John Ryan, married County Limerick, Ireland. (2) William Chuter, (widower) son of William Chuter, a timber merchant and Elizabeth Hammond. William Junior, a licensed victualler, Blue's Point, NSW. Married at St. Thomas' Willoughby, NSW 12 June 1863[86]
Children: Catherine Ryan and one boy and two girls not named on death certificate
Remarks: Lived about 11 years in colony of NSW. William Chuter married Susannah daughter of William/"Billy" Blue and wife Elizabeth in 1851.[87] Susannah Chuter died in 1861. Catherine's name

is on the list of 57 names compiled by Christian Brothers, Chatswood.

29. CHUTER, Catherine

Born: c. 1845, Ireland
Died: 16 June 1905[88]
Age: abt. 60 years
Buried: 17 June 1905, R.C. Cemetery, Chatswood
Father: Stephen/John Ryan
Mother: Catherine unknown
Spouse: (1) Thomas Robertson, a carpenter, married 11 November 1861 at Wesleyan Parsonage, Prince Street, Sydney.[89] (2) William Chuter (widower) born England, married Catherine Robertson at Elizabeth Street, (Presbyterian) in 1875.[90] He owned land at Berry's Bay, North Sydney and an inn with 'Billy' Blue at McMahon's Point. In March 1852 Susannah Lavender transferred the License for the *Macquarie Inn, North Shore* to William Chuter.[91]
Thomas Robertson, was son of Robert Robertson and Elizabeth McIntyre. Born in the colony. He died 25 September 1869,[92.] and is buried in St. Thomas' C of E Cemetery. William Chuter Senior died in 1882[93]
Children: 1st Marriage: Catherine born 1864, Thomas born 1865, Stephen born 1867.
2nd Marriage: 1. William Chuter, born and baptised at North Sydney Catholic Church in 1876.[94] 2. Henry born 1880.

30. COLLINS, Catherine/Katherine

Born: c. 1791
Died: 13 April 1872 at residence of son-in-law, *Union Inn,* North Shore[95]

Age: 81 years
Buried: Catholic Cemetery Chatswood
Father: John Roach
Mother: Mary unknown
Spouse: Jeremiah Collins of Anakassy, County Cork, Ireland
Children: Catherine, John, Francis (died 9 May 1886), Jeremiah
Remarks: Lived Pitt Water, NSW. Daughter Catherine married Bernard Daley proprietor of *Union Inn,* North Sydney. Jeremiah Collins Senior died at Pitt Water, in 1852 and his son Jeremiah Junior, died in October, of the same year.[96]

31. **COLLINS,** Francis
Born: c. 1825, County Cork, Ireland
Died: 9 May 1886, Barranjoey, NSW[97]
Age: 61 years, custom's boatman
C.O.D.: Heart disease
Buried: 11 May 1886, R. C. Cemetery, Lane Cove
Father: Jeremiah Collins, a government boatman
Mother: Kate, formerly Roach
Spouse: Eliza Graham married 1877/ Reg. No.1896, at Pitt Water, NSW
Children: no issue
Witnesses: Edward Connolly, James J. Roche
Remarks: arrived in colony on *Spitfire,* 2 January 1841.[98] Had resided 45 years in NSW. P.J. Collins, a nephew of Pitt Water registered the death.

32. **COLLINS,** John
Born: c. 1816, County Cork, Ireland
Died: 21 May 1881 at St. Leonards, late of Pitt Water[99]

Age: 65 years
Buried: Lane Cove R.C. Cemetery (SMH 23 May 1881)[100]
Father: Jeremiah Collins
Mother: Catherine unknown
Spouse: Honora Stanton, married 1847, St. Mary's Sydney. Honora died at Pitt Water 20 October 1897
Children: Margaret Mary, Katherine Mary (Roche), Jeremiah Joseph, Frank Edmund, Patrick John, Matthew Eneas
Grandchildren: John Theodore Swanson, Edmond Clements Swanson
Remarks: Lived Pitt Water NSW. Second daughter Margaret Mary died at *Union Inn,* North Sydney in 1863. John Collins was a signatory on 1865 Willoughby Petition.
His name is on list of 57 burials compiled by Christian Brothers, Chatswood.[101]

33. CONNERS/CONNOR, John/James Joseph
Born: 1851 NSW[102]
Died: 11 November 1886[103]
Age: abt. 35 years
Buried: Catholic Cemetery, Chatswood
Father: Michael Connor
Mother: Julia Quilligan
Spouse: Catherine Gallagher, married 1870 at Star of the Sea, Catholic Church, St. Leonards, 5 October 1870. Catherine was born County Fermanagh, Ireland and was daughter of James Gallagher and Jane Hardy of St. Leonards, NSW[104]
Children: Edward Alexander, baptised St. Mary's Ridge Street, North Sydney in 1879

Remarks: Lived Berry's Bay and worked as Alexander Berry's boatman.
Partial headstone extant. On the list of 57 burials compiled by Christian Brothers.

34. CONNERS/CONNOR, Julia
Born: c. 1820, County Limerick, Ireland
Died: 24 March 1870, at Berry's Bay, NSW[105]
Age: abt. 50 years
Buried: 26 March 1870
Father: Patrick Quilligan
Mother: unknown
Spouse: Michael Connor, married St. Mary's Sydney, 24 October 1837
Children: Mary (McKay), 30, Michael 29, John 27, Julia (Cole) 26, William, Bridget/Bedelia (Douglas) 20, James J. abt. 17 years.
Mary Connor born 1839, married Finlay McKay c. 1870, see **No.76**
Remarks: Julia Quilligan/Quillighan arrived in colony in October 1836 per *the Duchess of Northumberland*. She came free, was 22 years of age and a housemaid.[106] Deceased had lived about 34 years in the colony.

35. CONNERS/CONNOR, Michael
Born: c. 1805, Dublin,* Ireland
Died: 21 July 1884, Berry's Bay, St. Leonards, NSW[107]
Age: abt. 81 years
C.O.D.: Chronic diarrhoea
Buried: 23 July, 1884, North Willoughby Catholic Cemetery
Father: John Connor, a dairyman
Mother: Mary Kelly

Spouse: Julia Quilligan. Michael was granted permission to marry, Julia Quilligan/Judith Quiliken aka Julia Cunningham, in 1837[108]
Children: Mary (McKay) born1839, Michael born1840 married Sarah A Dunn, John born 1841, Julie (Cole/Coull) born1843, William born 1845 married Mary McHugh. Bedelia (Douglas) born 1847, 34, married James Hardie Douglas age 22 at Pitt Street, son of Alexander Douglas, a tailor and Anne Pattison, St. Michael's Sydney, 1869. James born 1851, married Catherine Gallagher, daughter of James Gallagher and Jane Hardy, 5 October 1870 at Star of the Sea, Catholic Church, St. Leonards
Remarks: Michael arrived per the *Sophia*, 17 January 1829.[109] TOL issued 3 June 1837, on condition he remain in the service of Mr Berry. Convicted of highway robbery and sentenced to transportation for life.[110] Michael Connor helped build a stone cottage overlooking Berry's Bay for his wife and seven children. *Convict record lists place of birth as County Meath, Ireland.
Witnesses: At funeral Michael Connor, William Connor

36. CONNOLLY, Eva Angela

Born: 4 July 1875, Barrenjoey, Pitt Water.NSW
Died: March 1878, at *Union Inn,* St. Leonards, NSW111
Age: abt. 2 years
C.O.D.: Diphtheria
Buried: 27 March 1879, Lane Cove Catholic Cemetery
Father: John Connolly, boatman Barrenjoey, born England c. 1828
Mother: Mary Agnes Collins, born Ireland, married Sydney, 1854
Witnesses: John Connolly, Frank Collins.

37. CONNOLLY, John

Born: c. 1830, London, England

Died: 17 February 1882, *Union Inn,* Lane Cove Road, North Sydney[112]

Age: abt. 52 years

C.O.D.: Chronic pneumonia

Buried: 18 February 1882, Lane Cove Catholic Cemetery

Father: John Connolly, grocer

Mother: Harriet unknown

Spouse: (1) Rebecca Devenish, married England, c. 1850, (2) Mary Collins, married Sydney 1854 St. Mary's Cathedral, Minister, Rev. J. J. Therry[113]

Children: 1st Marriage: Harriett (Mooney) 30. **2nd Marriage:** Jeremiah 25, William 23, John 21, Kate 19, Edward 18, Maria 16, Gregory 13, Gertrude 10

Witnesses: Jeremiah Connolly, R. Collins

Remarks: Lived approximately 23 years in New South Wales. First wife, Rebecca Connelly died in 1854.[114]

38. CONNOLLY, Mary Agnes

Born: c. 1828, County Cork, Ireland

Died: 19 October 1884, at Union Inn, St. Leonards[115]

Age: 56 years

C.O.D.: Paralysis from injuries received through a fall

Buried: 21 October 1884, Lane Cove Catholic Cemetery

Father: Jeremiah Collins, farmer

Mother: Katherine Roche

Spouse: John Connolly, married at age 26 years, St. Mary's Cathedral, Sydney in 1854. Rev. J.J. Therry officiated

Children: Jeremiah 27, William 25, John 23, Catherine 21, Edward 19, Maria 17, Gregory 15, Gertrude 12

Remarks: Resided about 44 years in NSW (SMH 20 Oct 1884).

39. **CONNOLLY, William Matthew**
Born: c. 1859, Sydney, NSW
Died: 1885, occupation blacksmith[116]
Age: abt. 26 years
Buried: 26 June 1885, Lane Cove Catholic Cemetery
Father: John Connolly, born England, c. 1828
Mother: Mary Agnes Collins
Witnesses: P.J. Connolly, J.F. Connolly

40. **COOKE, Ada Margaret**
Born: unknown
Died: 1872[117]
Age: infant
Buried: 19 May 1872, Lane Cove Catholic Cemetery
Father: John Henry Cooke, mariner, born Greenwich, England
Mother: Mary Ellis, (daughter of John Hammond and Mary Jones), married St. Mark's Anglican Church, Alexandria, Sydney, 1862[118]
Witnesses: William Porter, Richard Porter Junior
Remarks: John Cooke listed as undertaker. A John Cook was living at *Maryville,* Lane Cove Road, Turramurra, NSW.

41. **COSGROVE, Adolphus**
Born: 10 February 1868, at Miller Street, St. Leonards, NSW
Died: 10 February 1868, Miller Street, North Sydney[119]
Age: 1 hour - premature birth
Buried: 11 February 1868, Lane Cove Burial Ground (Chatswood)
Father: Thomas Cosgrove, a baker
Mother: Elizabeth Berkelman

Witnesses: Thomas Cosgrove, Abel Baldry

42. COSGROVE, Thomas

Born: c. 1819, Maclough House, County Cavan, Ireland
Died: 3 November 1871, at Miller Street, St. Leonards, NSW[120]
Age: abt. 52 years
C.O.D.: Ileuf
Buried: Chatswood R.C. Cemetery
Father: Thomas Cosgrove
Mother: Elizabeth/Bessie unknown
Spouse: Elizabeth Berkelman, married Sydney, 1854[121]
Children: Elizabeth born 1855, Anthony F. born 1856, Thomas born 1858, Frances born 1860, Mary born 1862, John born 1865 and Adolphus born/died 1868
Remarks: A member of first St. Leonard's Council and trustee of Catholic Burial Ground, Cooper's Flat, Chatswood. Brother-in-law to Patrick Freehill. Elizabeth Berkelman Cosgrove related to William Furlong Berkelman of Listowel Downs, Barcoo district, Queensland. Thomas Cosgrove's estate value at probate was 500 pounds.[122]
N.B. Partial headstone extant.

43. CUSICK, Timothy

Born: abt. 1828, County Clare, Ireland.
Died: 8 April 1893, at Orchard Road, Chatswood[123]
Age: 65 years
C.O.D.: Hepatic Cirrhosis, Diarrhoea
Buried: 10 April 1893, Chatswood Catholic Cemetery
Father: Patrick Cusick
Mother: not listed

Spouse: Catherine Lyons, married Westbury, Tasmania, 8 April 1856

Children: Bridget (Smith) 36, baptised Longford, Tasmania. Margaret (Betts) 32, Catherine Jane (Packer) 30, Elizabeth Ann (Windley) 23

Remarks: Lived four years in Tasmania and 36 years in NSW. Timothy left Tasmania for Sydney on 26 February 1857.[124] He was a signatory on Willoughby Municipal Petition in 1865. He owned a house and land on Lane Cove Road. His estate was valued at 820 pounds.[125] His occupation stated as retired farmer.

44. DALY, Bernard

Born: c. 1820, Hebbeggen, County Westmeath, Ireland
Died: 1 October 1877, West Street, St. Leonards, NSW[126]
Age: 61 years
C.O.D.: Apoplexy
Buried: 3 October 1877, Lane Cove Catholic Cemetery
Father: Matthew Daly, a farmer
Mother: Mary Geoghegan
Spouse: (1) Isabella Burnes/Beirne formerly McNulty, at St. Mary's Cathedral, 22 November 1853 by special licence, Isabella Daly died in April 1855.[127] (2) Catherine Collins, married St. Leonards, Catholic Church, 17 April 1856[128]
Children: Jeremiah 17, Bridget 15, Margaret 13, Mary 10, (4 deceased)
Witnesses: Thomas Manning, Patrick Kirby
Remarks: Bernard Daly resided in NSW for 36 years. He arrived per the *Pearl* 16 August 1841.[129] He was a publican and obtained the licence for the Union Inn, 26 March 1877.

45. **DALY**, Catherine

Born: c. 1830
Died: 7 October 1876, at Union Inn, North Shore, NSW[130]
Age: 46 years
Buried: 9 October 1876, Lane Cove Catholic Cemetery
Father: John Collins
Mother: Catherine Roche[106]
Remarks: No registration details found.

46. **DALY**, Mary Eleanor

Born: c. 1867, St. Leonards, NSW
Died: 9 August 1883, at Union Inn, Lane Cove Road, St. Leonards[131]
Age: abt. 16 years
C.O.D.: Disease of heart from rheumatism
Buried: 11 August 1883, Chatswood Catholic Cemetery
Father: Bernard Daly, publican
Mother: Catherine Collins
Witnesses: M. Connolly, P.T. Collins
Remarks: Frank Collins, uncle of Barrenjoey, registered the death.

47. **DALY**, Jeremiah Francis

Born: c. 1861, St. Leonard, NSW
Died: 30 March 1890, at West Street, St. Leonards[132]
Age: 29 years
C.O.D.: Phthisis
Buried: 31 March, 1890, Catholic Cemetery, Chatswood
Father: Bernard Daly, hotel keeper
Mother: Catherine Collins
Spouses: not married

Witnesses: D.H. Glacken, John F. Connolly
Remarks: Death registered by M.M. Daly, sister of deceased.

48. **DENNEHY**, Timothy Andrew
Born: 30 November 1900, Hunter Street, Hornsby, NSW[133]
Died: 6 February 1904, at Hunter Street, Hornsby[134]
Age: 3 years
C.O.D.: Diptheria
Buried: 8 February 1904, Chatswood Catholic Cemetery
Father: Timothy Dennehy, bricklayer, born County Kerry, Ireland
Mother: Bessie Maguire, born County Cavan, Ireland, married in Boston, America, 12 April 1891
Witnesses: John Walters, Walter Bruce
Siblings: In 1900, John 7, Mary H. 6, Maggie E. 4, Daniel P. 1 year
Remarks: Timothy Dennehy (father) was born County Kerry, Ireland.

49. **DONNELLY**, John
Born: c. 1847, North Shore, Sydney
Died: 18 December 1880, Little Arthur Street, East St. Leonards, NSW[135]
Age: abt. 31 years
Buried: 20 December 1880, Catholic Cemetery, Lane Cove, NSW
Father: William Donnelly
Mother: Mary unknown
Witnesses: Edward Donnolly and Thomas Byrne

50. **DONNOLLY**, John Willoughby
Born: 22 September 1867, Willoughby, NSW
Died: June 1869[136]

Age: 2 years
C.O.D.: Scarlatina
Buried: 25 June 1869, Roman Catholic, St. Leonards*
Father: Edward Donnolly, a labourer, also born Willoughby c. 1844
Mother: Lucy Daly, born Goulburn, NSW c. 1848
Siblings: Henry born 1866, Edward born 1869, Michael born 1871, Mary T. born 1874, Frederick W. born 1876, Albert born 1877
Remarks: *Catholic burials did not take place at Gore Hill until 1877. Edward Donnolly, listed on death certificate as undertaker.

51. DONNOLLY/DONNELLY, William

Born: c. 1822, Queens County, Ireland
Died: 15 December 1865[137]
Age: 45 years, a milkman
Buried: 17 December 1865, Catholic Ground North Shore
Father: Michael Donnolly
Mother: unknown
Spouse: (1) Mary Kelly married Sydney 30 September, 1840.[138] (2) Bridget Graham, married Sydney 1857. Bridget was born in Wexford, Ireland
Children: 1st Marriage: Edward 23, Patrick 21, John 18, Mary Teresa 15. 2nd Marriage: Catherine born 2 November 1859
Remarks: In April 1846 three of William's cows were shot and wounded by an unknown person.[139] In January 1865 William was ordered to pay wages to his employee for services performed in the capacity as milkman and gardener, of eighteen pounds seven shillings.[140]
Probate value of his property was 50 pounds.[141]

52. EBERT, Johann
Born: c. 1810, Niederheimbach on the Rhine, Prussia.
Died: 3 November 1870, West Street, St. Leonards, NSW[142]
Age: 60 years, gardener and vigneron
C.O.D.: Disease of the heart
Buried: 5 November 1870, Lane Cove Catholic Cemetery.
Father: Johann Ebert, gardener and vigneron
Mother: Katerina Wallemback
Spouse: Margaret Elizabeth Plat, married Neiderheimbach, Germany
Children: Catherine 29, John 28, Antony 26, Elizabeth 23, Mary 21, Frederick 13, Annie Anastasia 12, three children deceased
Witnesses: Antony Ebert, Jacob Roarman (sic)
Remarks: The family arrived per *Cateau Wattell* on 9 March 1855.[143] Johann, a gardener and vigneron, was employed by Alexander Berry. A Johan Ebert was naturalised in 1904/355. Mary Ebert married Peter Lanz/Lanff in 1874. The Lanff family was aboard the *Cateau Wattell* and also the Borig family (see No. 9 above). In March 1867 John Ebert sued John Fennessey over a fowl-house in West Street, St. Leonards. No order was made owing to the Bench disagreeing.[144]

53. EMMETT/HAMMETT, Christopher John
Born: c. 1867 England
Died: 14 February 1899, Victoria Avenue, Chatswood[145]
Age: 32 years
C.O.D.: Heart Disease, Syncope
Buried: Thursday 16 February, 1899, Cooper's Flat R.C. Cemetery Chatswood
Father: unknown
Mother: unknown

Spouse: Julia Alice Frost, married St. Stephen's Church, Willoughby, 1891.[146]

Julia Emmett, widow, married George A. Pobje in Sydney in 1899.

Children: no issue

Witnesses: Daniel (his brother), his uncles Richard McIlwain and Daniel Emmett/Hammett and Robert A. Emmett of Forest Lodge, his cousin

Remarks: Christopher arrived per the *Northampton*, with brother John in 1880.

Christopher Emmett was a land and estate agent in Victoria Avenue, Chatswood.

54. FENNESSEY, John

Born: c. 1835, Clonmel, County Tipperary, Ireland

Died: 20 February 1868.[147]

Age: 33 years

Buried: Chatswood Catholic Cemetery

Father: Edmund/Edward Fennessy/Fennessey

Mother: Margaret Kelly

Spouse: Catherine Lyons, born County Cork, Ireland. Married 19 February 1859, St. Leonards.[148] Her parents were James Lyons and Honora Condon

Children: one boy and three girls listed on death certificate Catherine born 1861, Margaret born 1864, Julia born 1868. Birth of son not found

Remarks: Rev. Fr. Peter Powell, Minister at marriage. A Mrs C. Fennessy was living at West Street, North Sydney in 1870. His name is on the list of 57 known burials compiled by Christian Brothers, Chatswood.

55. FLYNN, John
Born: 2 March 1866 at Erskine Street, Sydney[149]
Died: 12 July 1889, Kent Street, Sydney[150]
Age: 23 years
Buried: Catholic Cemetery, Lane Cove
Father: Patrick Flynn, a labourer, born County Cork, Ireland,
Mother: Margaret Reynolds born County Clare, Ireland

56. FLYNN, Margaret
Born: c. 1840, County Clare, Ireland
Died: 15 July 1889, at 461 Kent Street, Sydney[151]
Age: 49 years
Buried: 17 July 1889, Catholic Cemetery, Lane Cove Road
Father: Patrick Reynolds,
Mother: Catherine Neal
Spouse: Patrick Flynn, a watchman, married St. Mary's Church, Sydney, 1865[152]
Children: George 22, Margaret 18 years. One male (John) deceased
Remarks: claimed both County Clare and County Limerick as place of birth.
Resided 3 months in Victoria and 30 years in NSW
Witnesses: Patrick Flynn and Stephen Reynolds.

57. FLYNN, Patrick George,
Born: c. 1827, County Cork, Ireland
Died: 30 November 1891 at 5 Allen Street, Sydney[153]
Age: 64 years, night watchman
Buried: 2 December 1891, Lane Cove Catholic Cemetery
Father: Patrick Flynn

Mother: Catherine unknown
Spouse: Margaret Reynolds, married St. Patrick's Catholic Church, Sydney
Children: George 34, Margaret (Fletcher) 20, two males deceased
Witnesses: Albert Fletcher, Henry Dixon
Remarks: A. Fletcher, son-in-law, watchman, 5 Allen Street, Sydney registered the death.

58. **FORD**, Catherine
Born: March 1894, Sydney, NSW
Died: 5 July 1894, High Street, Willoughby, NSW[154]
Age: 4 months
C.O.D.: Congestion of the lungs
Buried: 7 July 1884 R.C. Cemetery, Chatswood
Father: Daniel Ford, a currier
Mother: Mary McGuiness, late Murphy
Witnesses: Daniel Ford, Donald Dukes.

59. **GAFFEY**, Elsie
Born: January 1902, Chatswood, NSW
Died: 24 January 1902, Archer Street, Chatswood[155]
Age: newborn 1 ½ days old
Buried: 25 January 1902, Cooper's Flat Cemetery, Chatswood
Father: Edward John Gaffey, a baker
Mother: Bessie Kelly/Kiely
Siblings: Lizzie born 1891, Lillian born 1892, Ellen M. born 1894, Edward born 1895, Bessie C. born 1897, Robert D. born 1903
Remarks: Family formerly lived at Glebe, Sydney before moving to Archer Street, Chatswood.

Witnesses: Edward J. Gaffey and Benjamin Leggett.

60. **GLOVER, Johanna**
Born: c. 1835, Ireland
Died: 10 October 1871, at Ridge Street, North Shore, Sydney[128]
Age: 36 years
Buried: Chatswood Catholic Cemetery
Father: Thomas Farrell
Mother: Mary unknown
Spouse: Henry Heath Glover, a lithographer, born Surrey, England, married Catholic Church, Tamworth, NSW 12 October 1856.
Children: Emily (Fibbens), Charles, Frank, Sydney Henry born 1871
Remarks: Henry Glover was the son of Henry Glover and Mary Ann Gerrard. Henry Heath Glover was a lithographer and his lithographs are in both the South Australian State Library and the Victorian State Library.
Henry (widower) married Jane E. Cliff/Clift at St. Thomas' Church, St. Leonards in 1873.[129] Henry Glover died 15 June 1904 at Oaks Street, North Sydney.
Her name is on the list of 57 burials compiled by Christian Brothers, Chatswood.

61. **GLOVER, Sydney Henry**
Born: 1871, NSW
Died: 17 October[130]
Age: an infant
Buried: Chatswood Catholic Cemetery
Father: Henry H. Glover, lithographic draftsman
Mother: Johanna Farrell

His name is on the list of 57 burials compiled by Christian Brothers, Chatswood

62. GOLDEN/GOULDING, Charles

Born: c. 1820, County Westmeath, Ireland
Died: 3 November, 1879, Arthur Street, East St. Leonards, NSW[131]
Age: abt. 63 years, drayman
Buried: Catholic Cemetery Chatswood
Father: Charles Golding
Mother: Mary Murray
Spouse: Elizabeth Cullen, née Hill. Married St. Mary's Sydney, c. 1850
Children: Mary 28, Margaret 26, John 24, Ann 22, Eliza 19, Jane 13.
Remarks: Charles Goulding's occupation was drayman. He was convicted of cow stealing in County Cavan on 28 February 1840 and sentenced to 10 years. His religion was catholic and he was single. Charles arrived on the *King William* on 17 August 1840.[132] Certificate of Freedom granted in March 1850. The family lived at 5 Little Arthur Street, North Sydney. In April 1856 he was charged with stealing 10 fruit trees from the garden of Frederick Arthur on the North Shore and sentenced to two months in gaol. In 1866 the family lived in Miller Street, St. Leonards.
His name Golden is on the list compiled by Christian Brothers, Chatswood.

63. GOLDEN/GOULDING, Elizabeth

Born: c. 1820, Gloucestershire, England
Died: 20 August 1907, at 5 Little Arthur Street, North Sydney[162]
Age: 84 years, nurse, old age pensioner
Buried: 23 August 1907, Catholic Cemetery Chatswood

Father: unknown Hill
Mother: unknown
Spouse: (1) Edward Cullen, born Louth, Ireland, married Melbourne, Victoria 1840
(2) Charles Goulding married St. Mary's Sydney, c. 1850
Children: 1st Marriage: Edward 63, born 27 December 1844, Manus, Goulburn NSW[163,] Ellen (Markwell) 58. **2nd Marriage:** Mary 56, Margaret 54 (Nelson/Nilson), John 52, Annie 49 (Somers), Elizabeth 47 (Beer)
Remarks: Elizabeth Hill convicted at Southampton April 1839 arrived per *Mary Ann* at Port Philip 1839, Convict No. 2248. Transported for seven years.[164] She was the owner of the house at 5 Little Arthur Street, North Sydney and her estate was valued at 310 pounds.[165] Deceased had lived in New South Wales c. 66 years. Daughter Elizabeth married Ross Donnelly Beer on 24 April 1878, at Scots Presbyterian Church, Sydney. Daughter Margaret Nelson of 59 Little Walker Street, North Sydney registered the death.
Elizabeth Golden is on list of 57 burials compiled by Christian Brothers, Chatswood

64.   GUINANE, Mary Kate (Kitty)
Born: c. 1881, North Sydney, NSW
Died: 5 November, 1904 at Kurring-gai (sic) House, Peat's Ferry Road, Waitara, NSW[166]
Age: 23 years, a domestic
C.O.D.: Phthisis
Buried: 7 November 1904, Catholic Cemetery Chatswood
Father: Cornelius Hisson Guinane, a draper (deceased), formerly of Avondale Street, Melbourne, Victoria
Mother: Margaret Teresa Campbell

Spouse: not married
Brother: J. Guinane, of 22 Carrington Street, Sydney registered the death
Witnesses: Benjamin Leggett, Robert Jackson

65. HARNETT, Margaret Sophia

Born: c. 1826, Kilrush, County Clare, Ireland
Died: 12 January 1868, at Gore Hill, Sydney[167]
Age: 42 years
C.O.D.: Convulsions
Buried: 13 January 1868, Catholic Burial Ground, North Shore (Chatswood)
Father: Simeon Sheehy, a builder
Mother: Ellen Donellan
Spouse: Richard Hayes Harnett, married 1847, Sydney, NSW
Children: Richard born 1850, Ellen born 1851, Sarah I. born 1854, Corada M., Agnes Kate,
Bessie, Rolla A., Cora A., Mary E.
Remarks: Margaret Sheehy aged 17 years and parents Simeon Sheehy 39 and Ellen 36 years, with children Daniel 9 and Mary 12, arrived per *The St. Vincent* on 31 July 1844. Richard H. Harnett, a native of County Cork, Ireland, arrived in the colony on the *China*, in 1840. He owned 1200 acres (485 ha) in Willoughby and subdivided much of Chatswood. He was mayor of Willoughby in 1868. Harnett also subdivided his land in Mosman. He purchased 108 acres (43 ha) from Archibald Mosman in 1859. Richard died aged 82 years at *Comeen,* his residence in Orchard Road, Chatswood in 1902.[168]
Partial headstone extant and on the list of 57 known burials.

66. **HARVEY**, William
Born: 30 November 1870, Eastern Creek, District of Penrith, NSW
Died: 30 August 1909, High Street, Willoughby NSW[169]
Age: 37 years, lorryman (tanner's), invalid pensioner
C.O.D.: Phthisis
Buried: 31 August 1909, Catholic Cemetery Chatswood
Father: William Harvey, a carpenter
Mother: Mary Sullivan, born Ireland
Spouse: Agnes Mary O'Connor, age 21 years, married 20 November 1893, at St. Nicholas Catholic Church, Penrith NSW. William Harvey was living at Rooty Hill
Children: Alan A. 15, Sylvester 13, Charles Roy 12, Hector N. 9, Harold N. 5
Witnesses: F.C. Holmes, W. F. Smedley
Remarks: S. Harvey, brother, Smith Street, Willoughby registered the death. William Harvey Senior was born in Newfoundland, c. 1816. He married Mary Sullivan in Sydney, 8 August 1854.

67. **HOWARD**, Lawrence
Born: County Clare, Ireland
Died: 27 July 1905, at Turramurra, NSW[170]
Age: abt. 98 years, orchardist, old age pensioner
Buried: 28 July 1905 Cooper's Flat Catholic Cemetery
Father: James Howard, a farmer
Mother: Margaret Scott
Spouse: not married
Remarks: Resided in NSW for 60 years. An associate of James Cherry of Gordon. His headstone inscribed 98 years while death certificate stated 87 years. Lawrence Howard, 30 years of age, arrived in the colony per *Alfred* in 1860.[171]

His name is on the list of 57 burials compiled by Christian Brothers, Chatswood.

68. **HOWARD**, Mary
Born: County Clare, Ireland
Died: 19 February 1908[172]
Age: 95 years
Buried: Cooper's Flat Cemetery, Chatswood
Father: James Howard
Mother: Margaret Scott
Spouse: not married
Remarks: Lived Lane Cove Road (Pacific Highway) Turramurra. Mary Howard's friend Mary Gilroy (wife of Peter Gilroy) was left a bequest in her Will. Mary Howard was referred to in James Cherry's Will as an employee. Arrived per the *Harriett* in June 1853 with two sisters.[173]

69. **JARVIS**, Louisa Irene
Born: 23 April 1901, at 40 Levy Street, Sydney.
Died: 11 October 1901, at 40 Levy Street, Sydney[174]
Age: abt. 6 months
C.O.D.: Bronchial catarrh
Buried: 13 October 1901, Catholic Cemetery Chatswood
Father: Frederick James Jarvis, a glazier
Mother: Matilda Ann Power, born North Sydney, married 8 September 1894 St Peter's C of E, Woolloomooloo, NSW
Siblings; Frederick J. 5, Nita L. 4, Myra O. 3.

70. **LOFBERG**, Clara
Born: January 1878, Happy Valley, Lane Cove, NSW[175]

Died: 27 October 1879 [176]
Age: infant (1 year 11 months)
Buried: Chatswood Catholic Cemetery
Father: Jonas Lofberg
Mother: Adeline Luis

71. **LOFBERG, Jonas Peter**
Born: Carlskrona, Sweden c. 1835
Died: 31 July 1880, Ryde Road, Lane Cove NSW[177]
Buried: 2 September 1880, R.C. Cemetery, Lane Cove
Father: Jonas Lofberg
Mother: Christina
Spouse: Adeline C. M. Luis, married 16 November 1863
Children: Helene, Cecilia (Blake), Jonas, Andrew P. George born1871 died 1872, Oscar Francis
Remarks: Deceased arrived in the colony from Sweden per *Cornelius Edward* in 1857. Jonas was naturalised in September 1869.[178] Jonas Lofberg's estate was valued at 350 pounds.[179] His son George was buried at St. Charles, Ryde, on 25 June, 1872.[180]
His name is on the list of 57 burials compiled by Christian Brothers, Chatswood.

72. **LYNCH, Andrew John**
Born: abt. 1879
Died: 10 February 1882[181]
Age: 2 years 2 months
C.O.D.: Croup
Buried: February 1882, Catholic Cemetery North Shore
Father: Patrick Lynch, special warden at Darlinghurst Gaol
Mother: Maria Jane Healey

Witnesses: Henry Mason Junior, J.C. Hillman

Remarks: No record found in Gore Hill Cemetery, assumed burial took place at Chatswood

73. **LYNCH,** Andrew Michael

Born: abt. 1887, Sydney, NSW

Died: 18 January 1890, at 459 Kent Street, Sydney, NSW[182]

Age: 3 years 8 days

C.O.D.: Diarrhoea

Buried: 19 January Catholic Cemetery, Lane Cove, NSW

Father: Patrick Lynch, letter carrier

Mother: Maria Healey

Witnesses: M. Hartmann, Henry Dixon

Remarks: No burial record found for Gore Hill Catholic Cemetery.

74. **LYNCH,** Hannah Theresa

Born: abt. 1881

Died: 31 October 1884, at 459 Kent Street, Sydney[183]

Age: 3 years 6 months

C.O.D.: Scarlatina

Buried: 1 November 1884

Father; Patrick Lynch

Mother: Maria Healey

Remarks: Patrick Lynch, police constable, age 24, married Maria Healey age 23 at St. Francis Church, Sydney on 15 January 1879. Patrick was born in Ireland the son of John Lynch and Bridget Reely. Maria Healey was born in New South Wales c. 1856, daughter of Andrew Healy and Anna Mackelcher (sic).

75. MCGLINCHEY, Margaret
Born: c. 1833, County Tyrone, Ireland
Died: 22 December 1897, at 518 Cleveland Street, Sydney[184]
Age: 64 years
C.O.D.: Acute Capillary Bronchitis, Cardiac Failure
Buried: 24 December 1897, R.C. Cemetery, Chatswood
Father: Hugh McHugh, provision merchant
Mother: Mary unknown
Spouse: Daniel McGlinchey, married Londonderry, Ireland
Children: Emily 43 (Wiles), John 42, Mary 39, Margaret 36, Ellen 33, Daniel 30
REMARKS: Margaret had lived 40 years in NSW. Death occurred at residence of son Daniel McGlinchey, 518 Cleveland Street, Sydney.

76. MCKAY, Mary
Born: c. 1839, St. Leonards, Sydney
Died: 25 February, 1877, at Domain Lodge, Riley Street, Sydney[185]
Age: 38 years
C.O.D.: Consumption
Buried: 27 February, 1877, Lane Cove Catholic Cemetery
Father: Michael Connor, Waterman
Mother: Julia Quilligan
Spouse: Finlay/Findlay McKay, married 9 November 1870 at St. James' Church, Sydney. Finlay McKay was coachman to Alexander Berry
Children: Anne Mary born 1871, Crow's Nest House, St. Leonards
Remarks: Partial headstone extant and name on the list of 57 known burials.

77. MACKELL, Hannah/Johannah
Born: c. 1841, County Limerick, Ireland
Died: 18 April 1901[186]
Age: abt. 67 years
Buried: Chatswood Catholic Cemetery
Father: Edmond Ryan
Mother: Mary Wickstead
Spouse: John Mackell, a labourer. Married St. Mary's Cathedral, Sydney, 26 August 1865. John Mackell, born c. 1843, County Fermanagh, Ireland, son of Michael Mackell and Catherine McDermott, lived in Kent Street, Sydney in 1865[187]
Children: Mary Ann Teresa
Remarks: Family lived in Stoney Creek, North Shore, Sydney. Funeral moved from opposite the public school, Pymble, NSW.

78. MCKELL, Mary Ann Teresa
Born: c. 1866, Sydney, NSW
Died: 16 September 1884[188]
Age: 17 years 6 months
C.O.D.: Consumption
Buried: 18 September 1884, North Willoughby Catholic Cemetery
Father: John Mackell
Mother: (Jo) Hannah Ryan
Witnesses: Dan Ryan, Martin Gibbon

79. MCMAHON, Ellen/Eleanor
Born: c. 1822, City of Cork, Ireland
Died: 26 February 1899, at *Traveller's Rest*, Pymble[189]
Age: abt. 80 years

C.O.D.: Senile decay, Exhaustion

Buried: 28 February 1899 Cooper's Flat Catholic Cemetery

Father: Eldest daughter of Thomas Boyd, a soldier in the Imperial Army, timber merchant in Sussex Street, Sydney

Mother: Ellen Roche, married Hadda, County Cork, Ireland, c. 1815

Spouse: Owen McMahon, born c. 1809, Sydney, NSW. Married c. 1834, Sydney

Children: William O. 64, Mary (Porter) 59, Ellen (Sullivan) 56, Thomas G. 54, Elizabeth (Harris) 48, Susan (Arthur) 46, James E. 42, Theresa (Wilson) 40, Annie 35, two males and one female deceased

Remarks: Ellen McMahon had resided in NSW about 73 years and was a generous benefactor to the Chatswood Catholic Church. Ellen's father, Thomas Boyd fought in the Peninsula War in Spain and arrived in the colony with the Royal NSW Veteran Company.[190] He was granted a Veteran's Allotment of 100 acres (40 ha) Section 410 in the parish of Gordon by Governor Darling. He named the property, *Toulouse Farm*.[191] Thomas Boyd Senior died at Mount Street, St. Leonards in 1858, age 66 years.[192] James Boyd, Ellen's brother, went to northern New South Wales in the 1840s in search of cedar. He and his family finally settled on the Tweed River.

80.   **MCMAHON**, Owen

Born: 1809, Female Factory, Parramatta, NSW[193]

Died: 1 December 1885, Gordon, North Shore, Sydney[194]

Age: 76 years, farmer

Buried: 3 December 1885, Catholic Cemetery, Chatswood

Father: *Said to be Owen McMahon, a convict per *Rolla* 12 May 1803

Mother: Ann Byrne – a convict arrived per *Rolla*, 12 May 1803[195]

Spouse: Eleanor/Ellen Boyd married 1834, NSW

Children: William O. 52 married Hannah Redgrave, in 1861; John 49 married Mary Foster, 1864; Mary 45 married Richard Porter III 1862; Ellen 42 married Edward A. Sullivan 1877; Thomas A. 40 married Ellen A. Maher 1870; Sarah A. 39 married William J. Porter 1869; Elizabeth 36 married Mr Harris, Susan 33; James E. 29 married Emily L. Smith 1881; Teresa 26 married Richard Wilson 1891; Annie 21 married (1) George V. McIntosh, 1890 (2) Joseph Robinson, 1899. One male deceased in 1885.

*Person certifying death gave father's name as John McMahon. Ann Byrne stated - Owen McMahon was the father of her child Owen born at the Female Factory.[196]

His name is on the list of 57 burials compiled by Christian Brothers, Chatswood.

81. MCMAHON, Thomas

Born: c. 1820, County Cork, Ireland
Died: April 1875, at Carr Street, St. Leonards[197]
Age: abt. 55 years
C.O.D.: Choleraic diarrhoea
Buried: 14 April 1875, Catholic Cemetery, Lane Cove
Father: John McMahon
Mother: Margaret McCarthy
Spouse: Hannah Lynch, married St. Mary's Sydney
Children: John 28, Thomas 24, two boys deceased
Witnesses: H. Coyle, J. Jolly
Remarks: His occupation stated as boatman.

82. MCMAHON, William Owen

Born: abt. 1835, New South Wales
Died: 3 March 1899 at Taree, NSW[198]

Age: 64 years
Buried: 8 March, 1899, Cooper's Flat, Chatswood
Father: Owen McMahon
Mother: Ellen Boyd
Spouse: Hannah Redgrave, married 31 August, 1861, St. Leonards[199]
Children: Mary E. born 1862, died August 1864; William T. born 1864; Mary E. born 1866; Hannah C. born 1868; Alice F. born 1871; Elizabeth born 1874
Remarks: The remains were brought back to Sydney on the North Coast Company's *SS Coraki,* from Taree where William (Billy) had owned the *Steam Packet Hotel,* later renamed the *Exchange Hotel.*[200] The *Steam Packet* burnt down in 1913. William McMahon was involved in horse racing and won several trophies with horses, *Satan, Exile* and *The Warder.* William built a racing track at his Pampoolah property and also a sawmill. Three of his daughters were excellent riders winning ribbons at the Sydney Show.[201]
His name is on the list of 57 burials compiled by Christian Brothers, Chatswood.

83. MALONEY/MOLONEY, Cornelius

Born: c. 1833 County Tipperary, Ireland
Died: 1 August 1888 at Gordon, NSW[202]
Age: abt. 55 years
C.O.D.: Paralysis of the heart
Buried: 3 August 1888, Cooper's Flat Cemetery, Chatswood
Father: Lawrence Maloney
Mother: Kate Hogan
Spouse: Ellen Gorman, married County Tipperary, Ireland c. 1857
Children: John who died before his father, no other children
Witnesses: A. Lemcke, A. Taylor

Remarks: Lived about 13 months in South Australia and 29 years in New South Wales. In 1878 Cornelius was a member of the Board of Roman Catholic Denominational School. In March 1857 Cornelius Maloney and Daniel Ryan were charged with ... cutting timber on Crown Land in the parish of Gordon and fined ten shillings ... An Inquest was held into his death.[203] The spelling was changed from Moloney to Maloney at the request of wife Ellen to correct death certificate.

84. MALONEY/MOLONEY, Ellen

Born: c. 1830, Ballywire, County Tipperary, Ireland
Died: 2 September 1896, Bobbin Road, Gordon, NSW[204]
Age: abt. 66 years
C.O.D.: Morbus Cordis
Buried: 4 September 1896, Cooper's Flat, Chatswood
Father: Phillip Gorman
Mother: Judith McNamara
Spouse: Cornelius Maloney, married c. 1857, Ballywire, Parish of Clonbeg, County Tipperary
Children: John who died 1867
Witnesses: T. R. Porter, Elizabeth King
Remarks: Lived Pymble and was 38 years in NSW. Funds from her estate were donated for an altar at Our Lady of Dolours Church, Chatswood. Ellen was aunt to Mrs James King and Alice Gorman. The name Maloney was initially registered as Moloney but changed to Maloney. Her name on extant list of 57 burials.

85. MALONEY/MOLONEY, John

Born: 1860, registered as Malone
Died: 15 February 1867[205]

Age: abt. 7 years 8 months
Father: Cornelius Maloney
Mother: Ellen Gorman

86. **MATHEW**, James Charles Crawford
Born: County Tipperary, Ireland, c. 1821
Died: 2 June 1868, Berry Street, St. Leonards[206]
Age: abt. 49 years
Buried: cemetery not named
Father: John Matthew/Mathew
Mother: Eliza Crawford
Spouse: Eveline Price, married Orange, NSW in 1866
Siblings: Brother to Ann Mathew Callen/Callan
Remarks: James, a saddler, was a nephew of Rev. Fr. Theobald Mathew, the Temperance Advocate in 19th century Ireland. Theobald Mathew was born at Thomastown Castle near Cashel, County Tipperary in 1790. He joined the Capuchin Order and preached temperance to crowds all over Ireland America and England. Memorial statues were erected in both Dublin and Cork. James Mathew arrived in the colony of NSW on the *Fairlie* together with five sisters.[207] **N.B.** Place of burial stated as St. Leonards. No record of a Catholic burial in St. Thomas' Cemetery so it appears that James Mathew was buried at Chatswood Catholic Cemetery with other family members.

87. **MULLONEY**, Peter
Born: c. 1816, Sydney NSW
Died: 30 May 1872[208]
Age: 56 years
C.O.D.: Albuminuria

Buried: 1 June 1872, Lane Cove Catholic Cemetery
Father: Joseph Mulloney
Mother: Catherine unknown
Spouse: Mary O'Connell, married abt. 1857, Sydney, NSW
Children: no issue
Witnesses: James Phelps and George Barnett
Remarks: His occupation was listed as waterman. Religion stated as Church of Christ. Minister at funeral, John Kenny.

88. MURPHY, John

Born: c. 1843, Ireland
Died: 4 May 1880[209]
Age: abt. 37 years
Buried: 5 May, 1880, Catholic Cemetery, Lane Cove
Father: Daniel Murphy
Mother: unknown
Spouse: unknown
Remarks: Lived about three years in New South Wales.

89. O'FLYNN, Rev. John P., Society of Jesus (S.J.)

Born: County Cork, Ireland
Died: 10 March 1881, at Berry Street Presbytery, North Sydney[210]
Age: 31 years
C.O.D.: Phthisis
Father: unknown
Mother: unknown
Remarks: John was a student priest and earlier had taught at St. Kilda Melbourne, Victoria.
The remains were reinterred in Gore Hill Cemetery.

90. O'GRADY, Margaret
Born: c. 1836, County Limerick, Ireland
Died: 10 July 1892[211]
Age: abt. 56 years
Buried: Cooper's Flat Cemetery, Chatswood
Father: Francis Taylor, a farmer
Mother: unknown
Spouse: (1) Patrick Reynolds married 1854, County Clare, Ireland. (2) William O'Grady, married 1882, NSW
Children: Michael, James, Mary (Slattery), Catherine, Anna, Bridget (Walsh), Patrick, Margaret, Honora, Francis, Stephen Reynolds. No issue second marriage
Remarks: Margaret left an estate valued after probate at 7,126 pounds.[212]

91. O'GRADY, William
Born: c. 1848, County Tipperary, Ireland
Died: 15 July 1887[213]
Age: abt. 40 years
Buried: 17 July 1887, Catholic Cemetery, Lane Cove
Father: Rody (Roderick) O'Grady, a farmer
Mother: Margaret unknown
Spouse: Margaret Reynolds née Taylor (a widow) age 41 years, married William O'Grady, a farmer, 28 October 1882, Berry Street, North Shore in a Roman Catholic ceremony[214]
Remarks: William had lived seven years in New South Wales. Patrick Reynolds, stepson of Gordon, Sydney, registered the death.

92. **OLIVER**, Mary,

Born: c. 1814, Port Stephens, NSW

Died: 12 July 1879[215]

Age: abt. 75 years

C.O.D.: Chronic bronchitis

Buried: 20 July 1879 at Catholic Cemetery North Willoughby, NSW

Father: unknown Brown

Mother: unknown

Spouse: William Oliver, married 1830, St. James' Church, Sydney, NSW

Children: William, Henry, Mary Ann (Archbold), Eliza, Emma, Thomas, Charlotte (Wilson), Louisa (Johnson)

Remarks: William Oliver was licensee of *Sawyer's Arms,* at Pitt Water, in 1840-41[216]

93. **PARFITT**, Frances

Born: 1 August 1851, Parramatta, NSW

Died: 14 May 1891, Gordon, Lane Cove, NSW[217]

Age: 39 years 8 months

C.O.D: Cancer of the Bowel

Buried: 16 May 1891, Cooper's Flat Cemetery, Chatswood

Father: William Burke, a farmer

Mother: Sarah Ann Corncrake/Conquit

Spouse: John Parfitt, married 22 September 1874, 163 Kent Street, Sydney

Children: Sarah Ann, born 1874

Witnesses: John Parfitt, Sarah J. Burke

Remarks: John Parfitt, a drummer in the Marines and wife Sarah arrived per *Prince of Wales,* with the First Fleet, 26 January 1788.

John was the son of George Parfitt and Eliza Walker. John Parfitt died c. 1891. His stated religion was Church of England.[218]

94. PENDERGAST/PRENDERGAST, John
Born: c. 1866, England
Died: 2 January 1885, at Hornsby, NSW[219]
Age: 19 years
C.O.D.: Struck by a stone thrown by Thomas Foster who was tried and found not guilty of manslaughter
Buried: Cooper's Flat Catholic Cemetery, Chatswood
Father: Michael Pendergast
Mother: Margaret Carson
Spouse: not married
Remarks: An Inquest was held followed by a trial. J.E. Bowden, Coroner's Report dated 7 January 1885, found: "John Pendergast, 19 years, born England, died Hornsby 2 January 1885 from the effects of a stone thrown at him. Charge: Manslaughter against Thomas Foster. Inquest on 2 March 1885, held at dwelling house of John Tibbett/Tebbett, *Junction Hotel,* Hornsby. Jurors: David Freestone, James Shelley, Edward Fuller Osborn, John Slater, Francis Clark, William W. Bankier, Henry W. Osborn, George Dunbar, John Leek, James Barry, Frederick Collins, Cornelius Cardigan." John Pendergast's father Michael, a labourer on the Great Northern Railway Works, at Hornsby, stated "My son John Pendergast, was employed on the same work ... He was alive at our tent. I went to Thomas Foster's place and ... *I looked at my boy's body.* Thomas Foster stated ... *I am married, have eight children born in district. I am 36 years of age. Mr Ready (is) my brother-in-law, my neighbour Mr Carpenter. I depend on my fruit for the support of my wife and family ...* John Pendergast (and another man Arthur Mayne) went to Foster's

orchard to eat some fruit, i.e., peaches. Thomas Foster was awakened by the noise coming from the orchard and threw a stone to chase them off. The workers on the (Homebush/Waratah) railway line often went to the orchard to eat fruit and a great deal was stolen. The railway line crossed Thomas Foster's land and his orchard was easily accessible to the railway line workers. Thomas Massey Harding, a medical practitioner of Ryde, gave evidence that in his opinion death came from a fall after John Pendergast was struck."[220] Thomas Foster was found not guilty of manslaughter at the Central Criminal Court. The case was widely reported in the newspapers of the day both in Sydney and country.[221] The Pendergast family consisted of Michael and Margaret, parents, six children, Mary, Ann, John, Jane, Elizabeth and Michael. All arrived per *La Hogue*, 21 October 1878. Both parents were born in Galway, Ireland and lived in Shropshire and in Lancashire England. SRA reel 2141.[222]

On extant list of 57 known burials as Prendergast.

95. **PORTER**, Clara Teresa
Born: Leeds, England
Died: 8 September 1909, Mater Hospital, North Sydney[223]
Age: 34 years
C.O.D.: Ectopic pregnancy
Buried: 9 September 1909, R.C. Cemetery, Chatswood
Father: Samuel Wilde, a waiter
Mother: Sarah Button
Spouse: Albert Sylvester Porter, married Pymble, NSW
Children: Alice E. 10, Albert S. 8, Reginald J. 5, none deceased
Witnesses: George Broomfield, John Bellamy

Remarks: Lived 30 years in NSW. Clara Wilde, age 1 year and parents Samuel 23, Sarah 22, arrived in Sydney, per *St. Lawrence,* in 1877.

96. PORTER, Ernest Francis

Born: May 1898, Turramurra, NSW
Died: 25 July 1898[224]
Age: 2 months
C.O.D.: Pneumonia, cardiac syncope
Buried: 26 July 1898, Cooper's Flat Catholic Cemetery, Chatswood
Father: Richard Owen Porter
Mother: Bridget Josephine Quinn
Witnesses: Richard Owen Porter, George Bromfield (sic)
Remarks: No minister officiated.

97. PORTER, Ernest Reginald

Born: 1895, St. Ives, NSW
Died: 18 July 1895, at St. Ives, Parish of Gordon[225]
Age: 1 month
C.O.D.: Bronchitis
Buried: 20 July 1895, R.C. Cemetery, Cooper's Flat
Father: William Owen Porter
Mother: Grace Sophia Mary Loveday
Witnesses. W.J. Porter Senior, Richard Owen Porter

98. PORTER, John Augustine

Born: 1877
Died: 3 February 1879 at Lane Cove, NSW[226]
Age: 1 year 8 months

C.O.D.: Enteritis
Father: William James Porter, a farmer
Mother: Sarah McMahon
Witnesses: William Porter, Richard Porter Junior

99. **PORTER,** John Augustine

Born: c. 1905, Pymble, NSW
Died: 26 April 1908, 204 West Street, North Sydney[227]
Age: 2 years 6 months
C.O.D.: Gastroenteritis, exhaustion
Buried: 27 April 1908, Cooper's Flat Cemetery, Chatswood
Father: William Owen Porter, quarryman
Mother: Grace Mary Loveday, married 3 March 1889. Daughter of Henry Loveday and Isabella Hudson
Other children of William O. and Grace: Sarah born 1890, William H. born 1892, Ernest B. born 1895 died 1895, Robert born 1897, Lawrence O. born 1900, Edward P.J. born 1903, Alfred J. born 1909
Witnesses: W.H. Kirby, R.F. Thomas

100. **PORTER,** John Joseph

Born: 10 April 1901
Died: 19 September 1901[228]
Age: infant son
Father: Thomas Edward Porter of Pymble, labourer
Mother: Margaret Elizabeth Stein, married Thomas E. Porter, in 1895
Remarks: Name is on list of 57 burials compiled by Christian Brothers, Chatswood

101. **PORTER**, Sarah Ann

Born: 29 March 1847, Lane Cove, NSW

Died: 11 June 1891 at residence Gardener's Arms Hotel, Gordon[229]

Age: abt. 44 years

Buried: 13 June 1891, Cooper's Flat Catholic Cemetery, Chatswood

Father: Owen McMahon

Mother: Eleanor Boyd

Spouse: William Porter, married 41 Burton Street, Sydney, Free Church of England, February 1869[230]

Remarks: Sarah's mother, Mrs McMahon, owned the Travellers Rest at Gordon.

102. **PORTER**, William James,

Born: 1848, NSW

Died: 2 June 1901, Paddington, NSW[231]

C.O.D.: Result of a fall in premises at Little Coombe Street, Paddington, NSW

Age: abt. 53 years

Father: Richard Porter II

Mother: Ellen Fitzgerald (formerly Connolly)

Spouse: Sarah Ann McMahon married 8 February 1869

Children: William O. born 1869, Edward A., James S., John A. born 1877

Remarks: Richard Porter I was born in Nottingham, England and the family can trace their ancestry back to the 16th century. Richard arrived on the *Surprise* 2nd Fleet and wife Mary Hutchinson came on *Mary Ann* in 1791 [232/233/234/235]

103. **POWER**, Michael John

Born: c. April 1835, Manning River, NSW

Died: 9 May 1880, Castlereagh Street, Sydney[236]
Age: abt. 45 years, publican
C.O.D.: Phthisis
Buried: 11 May 1880, Lane Cove Catholic Cemetery
Father: John Power, farmer
Mother: Elizabeth Oshay (sic)
Spouse: Mary Walsh, married St. Leonards 1864*[237]
Children: James born 1866, Matilda A. born 1869 died 1874, Ellen M. born 1871, Julia M. born 1872, Mabel F. born 1879
Remarks: *Note on marriage register ... The above marriage is now solemnised a 2nd time to satisfy qualms of conscience. Previously married to the same party some months since ...

104. POWER, Matilda Anne

Born: 1869, Lane Cove, NSW
Died: 17 March 1874, at Volunteer Hotel, North Shore, NSW[238]
Age: 4 ½ years
C.O.D.: Burns accidentally received
Buried: 19 March 1874, Catholic Cemetery, Lane Cove
Father: Michael John Power, a publican
Mother: Mary Walsh
Witnesses: W.T.S. Steele, William J. Sugden

105. RADKE, Henrietta Elizabeth

Born: 29 March 1865, Lane Cove, NSW[239]
Died: 22 October 1866[240]
Age: 19 months
Buried: a non-Catholic burial
Father: Albert Radke, a native of Germany, a tanner

Mother: Anna Mary Bogre
Remarks: Her father, Albert, owned a tannery with Ludowici at Burns Bay, Sydney.
Albert Radke was a signatory on the 1865 Willoughby Municipal Petition. Albert Radke died 22 December 1899 age 72 years, Anna Mary Radke (wife) died 10 February 1897, age 54 years and Mary Catherine (daughter) died 13 May 1896. All three were buried in Gore Hill Cemetery.

106. REYNOLDS, Francis
Born: NSW 1870
Died: 9 November 1872[241]
Age: 2 years
Father: Patrick Reynolds
Mother: Margaret Taylor born Kilrush, County Clare, Ireland
Name on extant list of 57 burials.

107. REYNOLDS, Honora/Nora
Born: c. 1866, NSW
Died: 16 June 1867[242]
Age: 18 months (infant)
Father: Patrick Reynolds
Mother: Margaret Taylor
Name on extant list of 57 burials.

108. REYNOLDS, Norah
Born: May 1870, Lane Cove, NSW
Died: 12 February 1871 at Lane Cove, NSW[243]
Age: 10 months
C.O.D.: Teething, no inquest, buried by order of Coroner

Buried: 14 February 1871
Father: Patrick Reynolds, a farmer
Mother: Margaret Taylor
Witnesses: Cornelius Moloney, Daniel Ryan
Remarks: Michael Reynolds brother registered the death. Undertaker William Turner.

109. **REYNOLDS,** James,
Born: c. 1858
Died: 13 May 1901, 24 Burton Street, Sydney[244]
Age: 42 years
Buried: 14 May 1901 Chatswood R.C. Cemetery
Father: Patrick Reynolds,
Mother: Margaret Taylor
Spouse: Elizabeth Wade, married 8 May 1901, 24 Burton Street, Sydney, R.C.[245]
Siblings: Patrick and Stephen Reynolds were brothers
Remarks: James Reynolds, a fruit grower of Lane Cove. Wife Elizabeth Wade was daughter of Stephen Wade and Elizabeth Jaques of Tarana, NSW.

110. **REYNOLDS,** Michael
Born: c. 1857, believed to be in Victoria
Died: 31 July 1877[246]
Father: Patrick Reynolds
Mother: Margaret Taylor

111. **REYNOLDS,** Patrick,
Born: c. 1822, County Clare, Ireland
Died: 15 October 1876, in Parramatta hospital[247]

Buried: unknown
Father: Patrick Reynolds
Mother: Catherine O'Neill
Spouse: Margaret Taylor, married Kilrush, County Clare, Ireland
Children: Michael, James, Mary (Slattery), Catherine, Anna, Bridget (Walsh), Patrick, Margaret, Honora, Francis, Stephen
Remarks: Arrived in colony on *Royal Charter* in 1856 with one-year-old daughter, Catherine, who died in 1857. The family went first to Ballarat, Victoria, where Patrick was a miner. They moved to New South Wales in 1857 on board the *Wonga Wonga*, a steam packet of 1,250 tons. The *Wonga Wonga*, was contracted to deliver a mail service to California in 1870.[248]

112. **RILEY, John**
Born: c. 1815, Manchester, England
Died: 4 February 1873, at Miller Street, St. Leonards, NSW[249]
Age: abt. 58 years
C.O.D.: Pulmonary Phthisis
Buried: 5 February 1873, Lane Cove Catholic Cemetery
Father: John Riley
Mother: unknown
Spouse: Mary Carmody, married St. Mary's Cathedral, Sydney, c. 1852
Children: Edward 20, Mary Ann 18, Elizabeth 12, John 9, Ann 7. One female deceased
Remarks: Occupation a shoemaker; lived 49 years in NSW.

113. **RILEY, Margaret**
Born: c. 1870, St. Leonards, NSW
Died: 10 December 1871, Mount Street, St. Leonards, NSW[250]

Age: 1 year old
C.O.D.: Convulsions
Buried: 11 December 1871, Lane Cove Catholic Cemetery
Father: John Riley, of Mount Street, St. Leonards, a shoemaker
Mother: Mary Carmody
Witnesses: Edward Riley, John T. Callon
Remarks: No Minister officiated, Undertaker: J.J. Higley

114. **ROBERTS,** Eveline Stewart
Born: 1879
Died: 1 January 1880, North Sydney, NSW[251]
Age: 9 months
C.O.D.: Infantile Cholera
Buried: 2 January 1880, Catholic Cemetery, Lane Cove
Father: John Roberts, telegraph officer
Mother: Christina Carmody
Witnesses: John Roberts, Abraham Baldry

115. **ROBERTS,** John Rankin
Born: July 1877, East St. Leonards, NSW
Died: 9 November 1877, Somerset Place, East St. Leonards[252]
Age: abt. 4 months
C.O.D.: Infantile Cholera
Buried: 9 November 1877, Catholic Cemetery, Lane Cove
Father: John U. Roberts, a government telegraph line inspector
Mother: Christina Carmody, married John U. Roberts at Church of All Saints, Church of England, Bathurst, NSW, 21 April 1874. Christina lived at Glanmire, Bathurst, NSW
Witnesses: at funeral, George Abel Baldry, Frederick Dew

Remarks: John U. Roberts was at Chambers Creek in 1874, when his occupation was stated as mining manager. John U. Roberts and wife Christina were buried at Gore Hill Cemetery.
George Abel Baldry lived at Victoria Avenue, Chatswood and could be called upon to act as Undertaker.

116. **ROBINSON, Annie Matilda**
Born: Pymble, Sydney
Died: 28 May 1908 Lane Cove Road, Pymble[253]
Age: 41 years, home duties
C.O.D.: Pulmonary Tuberculosis, Heart Disease
Buried: 30 May 1908, Cooper's Flat Catholic Cemetery
Father: Owen McMahon, hotel keeper
Mother: Eleanor Boyd
Spouse: (1) George V. McIntosh, a Melbourne jockey, married 1890. (2) Joseph Robinson, a fellmonger of Palmer Street, Sydney, in 1899[254]
Children: No issue
Remarks: Witnesses Richard Porter, Mrs Wilson, brother James McMahon, nephew Thomas McMahon, sister Ellen Sullivan.

117. **ROCHE, James Joseph**
Born: c. 1854 Co Cork, Ireland
Died: 26 November 1904, Bayview, Pitt Water, NSW[255]
Age: 50 years, farmer
C.O.D.: Syncope, Acute Gastritis
Buried: 28 November 1904, R.C. Cemetery, Chatswood
Father: John Roche, a farmer
Mother: Elizabeth Lisk

Spouse: Catherine Mary Collins, married at home of mother, *Rockvale,* Pitt Water, Manly, 18 April 1883, R.C. ceremony, D. Hanly, minister. Witnesses at wedding Frank E. Collins and Gertrude Connolly
Children: John 20, Elizabeth E. 18, Mary H. 16, Kathleen A. 15, Nano 12, Francis M.G. 9
Remarks: Deceased had lived 25 years in NSW.

118. RYAN, Matthew
Born: c. 1799, Toomevar, County Tipperary, Ireland
Died: 21 June 1879[256]
Age: 80 years
Father: Matthew Ryan
Mother: Mary unknown
Spouse: Winifred Kennedy, married County Tipperary, Ireland
Children: John Patrick married Clara Pocock, Patrick, Mary (Bercon), Ellen (Larkins), Johanna (Lyons), Winifred (McMahon), Margaret, Bridget (McClelland)
Remarks: Matthew arrived per *Boanerges* in 1857 and lived 27 years in the Colony of NSW.[257] His daughter Ellen Larkins died 11 December 1885 at Mount Street, St. Leonards and was buried at Gore Hill Cemetery, North Sydney.
His name is on the list of 57 burials compiled by Christian Brothers, Chatswood.

119. RYAN, Winifred
Born: c. 1809, County Tipperary, Ireland
Died: 23 June 1889, at residence of daughter Winifred McMahon, Elizabeth Street, North Sydney, NSW[258/259]
Age: 80 years

Buried: 25 June 1889, Cooper's Flat Cemetery
Father: unknown Kennedy
Mother: unknown
Spouse: Matthew Ryan, married County Tipperary, Ireland
Witnesses: John McMahon and J.P. Ryan
Remarks: Winifred lived at Elizabeth Street, Victoria, North Sydney in 1888.

120. SCULLY, Francis
Born: January 1897, Willoughby, NSW
Died: 12 November 1897, Victoria Avenue, Willoughby[260]
Age: 10 months
C.O.D.: Acute Meningitis
Buried: 13 November 1897 R.C. Cemetery, Chatswood
Father: James Scully, a carter, lived Victoria Avenue, Willoughby NSW
Mother: Mary Clement
Witnesses: J. Scully, Albert Bugden
Remarks: The Scully family first settled at Camden, NSW then Prospect before moving to Willoughby, NSW. No minister of religion in attendance.

121. LATTERY, Mary
Born: c. 1859, Pymble, NSW
Died: 25 December 1897, at 24 Burton Street, Sydney, NSW[261]
Age: 38 years
C.O.D.: Tubercular Phthisis
Buried: 27 December 1897, R.C. Cemetery, Chatswood
Father: Patrick Reynolds, fruit grower

Mother: Margaret Taylor
Spouse: William Slattery, married Pymble, NSW, 1886
Children: William P. 10 years, born Moore Park Hotel, Bourke Street Sydney
Witnesses: William Farrell, Norman Blake

122. SLATTERY, William,

Born: c. 1859, County Tipperary, Ireland
Died: 21 December 1889, 461 Kent Street, Sydney[262]
Age: 30 years
C.O.D.: Phthisis
Buried: 23 December 1889, R.C. Cemetery, Lane Cove
Father: William Slattery a Farmer
Mother: Mary Ann Ryan
Spouse: Mary Reynolds, married R.C. Church, Lane Cove, 27 October 1886[263]
Children: William 2 ½ years, born 26 August 1887. Bourke Street, Sydney[264]
Witnesses: Edward Brown, Henry Dixon
Remarks: William Slattery, a Publican, had resided 10 years in NSW.

123. SWANSON, Ellen

Born: c. 1848
Died: 6 October 1874[265]
Age: 26 years
Buried: Catholic Cemetery, Chatswood
Father: John Collins
Mother: Ann

Spouse: Charles J. Swanson, a shipwright, of Pitt Water, married in R.C. Ceremony, at Pitt Water, 4 February, 1869[266]
Children: John Theodore and Edmund Clement
Remarks: Charles J. Swanson, widower, married Margaret Boyd, in 1881.

124. **TWEEDY, William John**
Born: c. 1830, Newry, County Down, Ireland
Died: 4 May 1908, at Royal North Shore Hospital, St. Leonards, NSW. Death registered by Matron A. M. Goddard of RNHS Hospital[267]
Age: abt. 78 years, orchardist
C.O.D.: Ileo Colitis
Buried: 6 May 1908, R. C. Cemetery, Chatswood
Father: not stated
Mother: not stated
Spouse: None stated on death certificate. William J. Tweedy married Mary Darcy at Bathurst C of E in 1853. Mary's father and mother George D'arcy/Darcey and Margaret O'Donnell were convicts[268]
Children: none stated on death certificate. Descendants claim there were eight. One son Robert Patrick Tweedy was a councillor on Dubbo Council
Remarks: Convicted in 1847 of stealing three silver spoons and transported for seven years arriving per *Havering* from Dublin in 1848. He was 19 years of age when granted a Ticket of Leave in 1849. He became a successful miner at Ophir, NSW. William separated from his wife and family about 1874. His family stated on his son's marriage certificate that he was deceased in 1897. William purchased land at Waitara and later at Hornsby where he established an orchard. Lot 13/DP 2561 County of Cumberland. William also

owned two properties at Prince Street, Balmain, sold in 1898. Robert Bartlett, author of *Ophir Gold* noted that William was a successful miner. William Tweedy was buried with a full Requiem Mass. Rev. P. Briody arranged the funeral through W.N. Bull. William bequeathed his estate to the Catholic Church to be used for the Sisters of Mercy Orphanage and the building of Waitara Catholic Church.[269]

125. **VOS**, Jacob Martinus
Born: 25 July 1846, Tilburg, Netherlands
Died: 1 October 1910, Anderson Street, Chatswood[270]
Age: 64 years
C.O.D.: Growth in stomach
Buried: 4 October 1910, R.C. Cemetery, Chatswood
Father: Martinus Joseph Vos, of independent means
Mother: Maria Verheyen (sic) Verheijden
Spouse: Margaret Dora Pammenter, a nurse, married at Randwick, NSW in 1898[271] Margaret was born in Midhurst, England c. 1861 and in charge of a Private Hospital *Francis* in Anderson Street, Chatswood abt. 1908 into the 1920s
Children: One son John and two adopted children, Joseph Thomas and Iris. Margaret Vos, widow, married John P. Mason of Vale, Denmark, in 1913.[272] Margaret Mason died 17 June 1927 at Chatswood
Remarks: Martinus Vos was a tobacconist and importer of cigars.

126. **WHITE**, John
Born: c. 1804, County Limerick, Ireland
Died: 5 January 1883, at Ridge Lane, St. Leonards, NSW[273]
Age: abt. 78 years

C.O.D.: Haemorrhage from Gastric Ulcer
Buried: 7 January 1882, Catholic Cemetery, North Willoughby, NSW
Father: Michael White
Mother: not stated
Spouse: Catherine Healey, married Ireland
Children: Margaret (Robertson) 40, Ann (O'Neill) 37, Kate 35, Elizabeth 32, Mary 29, Michael 27 living, two boys deceased
Witnesses: Henry O'Neill, John Callaghan
Remarks: John White was a labourer and had lived over 40 years in NSW.

127. **WILES, Emily,**
Born: County London Derry, Ireland.
Died: 18 September 1875 at Armidale, NSW[274]
Age: abt. 39 years
C.O.D.: Pulmonary Phthisis
Buried: 20 September, 1875, R.C. Cemetery, Lane Cove*
Father: Daniel McGlynchy, a baker
Mother: Not stated but believed to be Margaret McHugh
Spouse: Lewin Wiles, master mariner, and whaling Captain
Children: William, Lewin, Louisa, Isabella, John J., Ada
Remarks: Lived about 17 years in NSW. Mrs Wiles and son were passengers on the 300 ton Barque, *Australian* landing in Port Jackson, NSW from a whaling voyage on 12 May 1852 and passengers on a second voyage from The South Seas arriving in Sydney, NSW, 23 January 1854.[275] Captain Lewin Wiles died at Oak Cottage, Bray Street, Neutral Bay, in 1894 and was buried in St. Thomas' C of E Cemetery, North Sydney.[276] Emily's mother,

Margaret McGlynchy was buried at Chatswood Catholic Cemetery, 22 December 1897.

*No record found of how the remains were brought from Armidale for burial two days after her stated date of death.

Emily's name is on the list of 57 burials compiled by Christian Brothers.

128. **WILLOUGHBY**, William
Born: c. 1837, Bolton, Lancashire, England
Died: 2 September 1881, at North Willoughby, NSW[277]
Age: 43 years, jeweller
C.O.D.: Cirrhosis of Liver
Buried: 4 September 1881, Roman Catholic Cemetery, Willoughby
Father: Cornelius Willoughby
Mother: Susannah unknown
Spouse: Sarah J. Barnard, married Windsor, England, 1861 in December Quarter (1861 Census)[278]
Children: John William, William, Bradley/Bradleigh, James, John Henry, sons. No daughters stated
Remarks: William owned brickworks with son Bradley at Jacques Street, Willoughby. His occupation stated as jeweller. William left Windsor, England in 1879, and had lived in New South Wales for 2 years 3 months. William's Estate was valued at 4,364 pounds. Executor was Francis Bede Freehill. He left legacies to John Willoughby Read, his nephew and Charles Henry Seymour of Windsor, Berks. England.[279] John Henry Willoughby, his son, was living in London at time of father's death. The 1871 Census places William Senior living in Bolton, Lancashire with wife Sarah J. Barnard, born Southampton.[280] William's occupation: watchmaker. A non-Catholic burial.

An advertisement in the SMH dated 15 September 1881, on behalf of William Willoughby's estate, may provide an insight into the lifestyle of a well-to-do gentleman of that era.

Household effects: Watchmaker's tools of trade, pianoforte, water cooler, oil painting, Duchess suite, mangle and washing machine, sewing machine, hot water machine, trunks, portmanteau, chiffonier, horsehair couches, safe, clock, chest of drawers and clothing.

SUPPLEMENTARY LIST

1. COLLINS, Honorah

Born: c. 1819, Castle Town, County Cork, Ireland
Died: 20 October 1897, Bayview, Pitt Water, NSW
Age: 78 years
C.O.D.: Gangrene
Buried: 21 October 1897, R.C. Cemetery, Cooper's Flat, Chatswood
Father: Patrick Staunton, a miller
Mother: Ellen Mary Coleman Kirby
Spouse: John Collins, married Sydney, NSW
Children: Jeremiah 46, Katherine M. (Roche) 44, Francis 42, Patrick 41, Mathew 38
Witnesses: W.H. Kirby, R. F. Thomas, Rev. Fr. Patrick Dowling, R.C. Minister. Deceased had lived 57 years in NSW
Remarks: Elizabeth Kirby, Undertaker.

2. COOKE, Marian Ellen

Born: c. 1833 County Tyrone, Ireland
Died: 12 January 1907, *Rose Cottage,* Lane Cove Road, Turramurra

Age: 74 years
C.O.D.: Nephritis, Cardiac failure
Buried: 14 January 1907, Cooper's Flat, Chatswood
Father: unknown Higgins
Mother: unknown Morris
Spouse: John Cooke
Children: John 48, Andrew 42, George 40, Theresa 46, Mary 44 (Mrs Frank Johns)
Witnesses: John Cooke, John Cooke Junior, Rev. P. Briody, R.C. Minister
Remarks: Deceased had lived 54 years in NSW.

3. **CURTIS**, Frances Emily
Born: Pennant Hills, NSW
Died: 4 July 1902, Thomas Street, Chatswood
Age: 20 years 10 months, domestic servant
C.O.D.: Peritonitis, ruptured abscess of fallopian tube
Buried: 6 July 1902, Cooper's Flat Cemetery
Father: George Curtis, orchardist
Mother: Isabella Jenkins
Spouse: not married
Witnesses: George Curtis, Benjamin Leggett, H.C. Goldrick
Remarks: Granddaughter of Mrs M.E. Jenkins, John Jenkins, an uncle of 88 William Street, North Sydney registered the death.

4. **DRUITT**, Joseph
Born: c. 1863, Lane Cove District, NSW
Died: 1 September 1890, Coyle's Building, Miller Street, North Sydney

Age: 27 years, manager of a restaurant
C.O.D.: Phthisis
Buried: 2 September 1890, R.C. Cemetery, Cooper's Flat, Chatswood
Father: Joseph Druitt, mechanical engineer
Mother: Eliza Walsh
Spouse: Not married
Witnesses: William Druitt, James Druitt, Rev. Fr. Joseph Brennan
Remarks: William, James and Edward Druitt were brothers. Mrs Power and Miss
Walsh were aunts. John J. Power and James Power were cousins.

5. **FLYNN, George**
Born: c. 1868, Sydney, NSW
Died: 7 November 1893 at his residence 335 Harris Street, Pyrmont
Age: 25 years, labourer
C.O.D.: Acute Phthisis
Buried: 8 November 1893, R.C. Cemetery, Chatswood
Father: Patrick George Flynn (deceased), a watchman
Mother: Margaret Reynolds (deceased)
Spouse: Not married
Witnesses: Margaret Fletcher (wife of Albert Fletcher brother-in-law), David Doyle
Remarks: Rev. Fr. M. McNamara, R.C. Minister, officiated.

6. **MCMAHON, John**
Born: Lane Cove, Gordon
Died: February 1891 at Traveller's Rest Hotel, Gordon
Age: 54 years, sawyer

C.O.D.: Heart Disease
Buried: 18 March 1891, Cooper's Flat Chatswood
Father: Owen McMahon, farmer
Mother: Ellen Boyd
Spouse: Mary Foster
Children: John 25, Richard 23, Thomas 21, all living
Witnesses: James McMahon, Theresa McMahon.

7. **MULLANE**, Michael
Born: c. 1862, County Limerick, Ireland
Died: 22 April 1909, Wondabyne, Hawkesbury River
Age: 47 years, a railway labourer
C.O.D.: Accidentally run over by a train
Buried: 24 April 1909, R. C. Cemetery, Chatswood
Father: John Mullane, farmer
Mother: Anne Nolan
Spouse: Mary Mullins, married Sydney NSW, c. 1877
Children: John 14, James 12, Bernard 7, Michael 4
Witnesses: Michael Mullins, George Broomfield
Remarks: Lived 25 years in NSW. An inquest was held at Brooklyn, 23 April 1909, death registered at Gosford, 29 April 1909.

8. **NOONAN**, Patrick
Born: c. 1830, County Clare, Ireland
Died: 15 October 1898. Railway Avenue, Wahroonga
Age: 68 years, a dairyman
C.O.D.: Senile decay, Diarrhoea, Exhaustion
Buried: October 1898, R.C. Cemetery, Cooper's Flat, Chatswood
Father: Dennis Noonan, a farmer

Mother: unknown
Spouse: Margaret Ryan, married Sydney, NSW
Children: Mary 18, Agnes 16, May C.R. 13, William J. 9, Patrick 6, James 4
Witnesses: E. Morley, A. Roberts
Remarks: Had lived 42 years in NSW. R.C. Minister Rev. Michael Kirby.

9. PORTER, George John

Born: c. 1870 Pymble, NSW
Died: 9 June 1910, *Woodstock,* Fletcher Street, Marrickville
Age: 40 years, labourer Water & Sewerage Board
C.O.D.: Pulmonary tuberculosis
Buried: 11 June 1910, R.C. Cemetery, Chatswood
Mother: Mary McMahon
Father: Richard Joseph Porter, orchardist
Spouse: Gertrude Dowton, married Newtown, Sydney, NSW
Children: None stated
Witnesses: H. Field, B.F. Carroll
Remarks: William Dowton, father–in–law. George was brother to Agnes and Cis. R.C. Minister Rev. John Rohan. Undertaker: F. Dangar & Company

10. ROBINSON, Hannah

Born: Queens County, Ireland
Died: 25 December 1883, 6 Beauchamp Lane, off Gipps Street, Sydney
Age: 84 years
C.O.D.: Chronic Alcoholism
Buried: 27 December 1883, Catholic Cemetery, Lane Cove Road

Father: unknown McDonald
Mother: Alice (surname not listed)
Spouse: (1) William Beer married age 19, Sydney. (2) Frederick Robinson married Sydney
Children: 1st Marriage: 2 males, 2 females living. 2nd Marriage: 1 male living. Ross Beer, William Robinson, Fred Robinson - her sons named in Funeral Notice
Witnesses: James Gleeson, John Smith
Remarks: Deceased had lived 68 years in colony of NSW. No minister of religion listed.

11. **SWANSON**, Edmund Clement
Born: Pitt Water, NSW
Died: 28 December 1901, St. Vincent's Hospice, Victoria Street, Sydney
Age: 29 years, schoolteacher
C.O.D.: Pulmonary tuberculosis
Buried: 29 December 1901, R.C. Cemetery, Chatswood
Father: Charles J. Swanson shipwright
Mother: Ellen Collins
Spouse: Not married
Witnesses: W.H. Kirby, R.F. Thomas
Remarks: J.T. Swanson of 32 West Street, North Sydney, his brother.

Waitara Foundling House 1899-1997

Several parishioners of Chatswood Catholic Parish expressed the belief that little children who had died at the Waitara Foundling Home, in the late nineteenth and early twentieth centuries, were buried in Chatswood Catholic Cemetery. The sensitive records of the Home, which closed in 1997, were not public record and there didn't appear to be any way to prove or disprove this claim. It has now become possible to locate the names and burial details of 30 of those little children. With the passage of time, more than one hundred years after these burials took place, surely now, is an acceptable time to include this information. The practice of placing children, many of whom were illegitimate, in Foundling Homes is an important chapter in our country's social history. The secrecy surrounding their births and deaths meant that very few people knew of either, and tragically, even the mothers may never have known of their children's fate. It is hoped that no living person will be distressed by this attempt to acknowledge and memorialise these events.

In a Report to a meeting of the Sydney Benevolent Asylum committee, submitted by the Manager, Edward Maxted and published in the *Sydney Morning Herald*, 10 February 1891 he stated: "During the past 5 weeks no fewer than 6 abandoned infants had been received into the Asylum. Indeed the evil of infant abandonment seemed to be growing."[281]

At an earlier meeting held on 8 October 1890, on the subject of baby farmers, Mr Maxted commented: " ... an extensive traffic in infants continues to be carried on in this community." He continued: " ... it was proved in many instances of the 32 deserted infants received into the Asylum the desertion was traceable to baby farmers ... "

He further claimed that baby farmers made a livelihood accepting infants from their mothers for sums of money and then abandoning them in public places or distributing these infants to unsuspecting families, with the promise of payment for maintenance. The baby farmers then disappeared. He further deplored the practices of some owners of private lying-in homes. The management of the Society urged the Government to enforce the registration of private lying-in homes. The work of the Benevolent Asylum, and its care and assistance to families in need, was respected and acknowledged in the wider Sydney community. At its annual meeting in January 1890 it was reported that: "The number of cases investigated weekly in 1888 was 488 while in 1889 the figure increased to 507. The number of foundlings admitted was 18 as against 22 in the previous year. The number of destitute women and children admitted was 850 and the number admitted to the Lying-in Department was 261. A large number of infants were admitted in a dying or hopeless condition."[282]

Edward Maxted advocated for child protection laws to be introduced as a matter of urgency. In 1892 an Act was passed and remained in force for 10 years until 1902. The Act made it unlawful to adopt, rear, nurse or otherwise raise a child under the age of three for payment, without authorisation from a Justice of the Peace.

The publicity surrounding the trial of two baby farmers, John and Sarah Makin in 1892, exposed the magnitude of the suffering of both mothers and children over a long period of time. In 1892 Sydney police began an investigation into John and Sarah Makin, baby farmers, after workmen found the remains of two infant children in the backyard of their home in Burren Street, Macdonaldtown. Police went on to exhume the remains of infants from eleven houses previously occupied by the Makins. A total of twelve dead bodies were found. The Makins had been taking babies into care in exchange for cash payments, usually about 10/- (ten shillings) per week and in some cases with an initial payment of three pounds. John and Sarah Makin were arrested and charged with murder. At their trial Prosecutors alleged the Makins agreed to care for infants but found it easier to kill the children and continue receiving childcare payments. The mother of one of the children, 18-year-old Amber Murray, was able to identify the clothing of her dead baby, Horace Murray and gave evidence at the trial. Murray had placed an advertisement in the *Sydney Morning Herald* in 1892, seeking a mother to adopt a baby boy. The Makins replied and offered to take care of baby Horace in exchange for 10 shillings per week. They were given an initial sum of 3 pounds. A second couple's child, Minnie Davis and Horace Bothomley, died while in the care of the Makins. John Makin had been given two pounds to bury the infant and register the death. But John Makin was accused of keeping the money and neither registering the death nor burying the baby and in addition pawning the infant's clothes. The Makins were found guilty on the evidence of several witnesses, including their own daughters, Blanche and Florence Makin. John Makin was hanged and Sarah sentenced to life imprisonment.[283]

The publicity surrounding the Makin's trial soon enabled Mr Sydney Maxted, chief officer under the Children's Protection Act of 1892, to discover and have prosecuted other baby farmers. Annie Robina Rooke was charged with having received into her care, Roy Stacey, without a written order of a Justice. Ms Rooke in evidence stated that she had received eight pounds to keep the boy and ... gave him out for three (pounds) ... Emma Tracey, a single girl, residing at Albermarle Street, Paddington stated ... she was delivered of a male child in July 1892. She inserted an advertisement for someone to adopt a child and the accused answered it. Emma Tracey took the child to Rooke's house at Waterloo who said she would adopt the child and treat it as her own. Rooke was paid eight pounds for which a receipt was given and the baby was left with Rooke.[284]

At that time many people in the Catholic community of Sydney became more aware and concerned at the high rate of infanticide as well as the ill-treatment and rejection of unmarried mothers. The women became outcasts from society particularly in the 1890s. This decade was a time of severe depression and the abandonment of babies was evidence of society's rejection of unmarried mothers, possibly exacerbated by widespread poverty. St. Anthony's Hospital in Surry Hills was established to meet this need but it soon proved inadequate owing to the large numbers of victims, both women and children. At the government-funded Ashfield Infant's Home, Catholic inmates could not receive the sacraments and all babies were baptised by Protestant clergymen. Cardinal Moran sought a solution and appealed to the Sisters of Mercy at North Sydney to assist by establishing a Foundling Home on the North Shore. At the Cardinal's urgent request, the Sisters agreed to delay building their proposed hospital at North Sydney. From 1895 until 1897 the Sisters of Mercy cared for foundlings at Lane Cove Road, North Sydney.

The foundation stone, for a new Foundling Home at Waitara, was laid and blessed in April 1898 and the official opening took place in May 1899. The architect, H.B. Wadell designed the home to accommodate 100 infants. The initial intake was 70, increasing to 84 by 1900. The Foundling Hospital was non-sectarian in its operations. The Cardinal provided 10 acres (4 ha) of land at Waitara and an orchard, including a cottage, owned by Charles Leek Junior, was purchased giving the Mercy Order an area of approximately 37 acres (15 ha). The cottage became a Hospice for the Dying.[285] Initially some residents of the area were unhappy with the establishment of a Foundling Home and feared it would bring disease and 'fallen women' to the area. In the early years the rate of infant mortality was found to be high at 30 per cent, as stated in the first annual report of 1900.[286] The majority of the deaths being due to atrophy; half of these deaths occurred within days of the infants being admitted to the Home. Twenty children had been removed by their mothers. The home gave shelter to 30 destitute and sick mothers and 20 of these were found situations. To solve the problem of the high death rate, facilities were then provided for mothers to stay and care for their infant children.

In one 12-month period 365 stillbirths were registered in New South Wales. The Foundling Hospital became a home for unmarried mothers and their babies. The first Superior of the Mercy Order to take charge was M. Aloysius Casey. All of this charitable work was undertaken to alleviate the suffering of abandoned women and children and as a means of reducing the rate of infanticide. A newspaper article in 1910 reported that a three-week-old baby boy was found abandoned in the Catholic Church in Upper Pitt Street, North Sydney. The baby was described as 'thin and poorly nourished.'[287] He was taken to the Waitara Home. In the same year there were two more reports of babies being abandoned at Catholic Churches, one at Lewisham and another at St. Patrick's Church Hill, Sydney. Margaret Smith, a 17½-year-old domestic servant was charged with abandoning her baby, Millie Smith, at Waitara Station Waiting Room in April 1900. The young mother stated that she was unable to support her baby and in desperation took her to Waitara.[288] In March 1910 Vincent Flynn was found at Milsons Point, North Sydney and died at the Waitara Home of gastroenteritis, in April of that year. He was two months old.[289]

A lay committee was formed to oversee the work of the Home and the wives of John and James Toohey were early members. Mark Foy made generous contributions towards the setting up and running of the Home. Mrs Hughes and Miss O'Brien were joint secretaries. There was a change of name in 1952, when the Foundling Hospital became known as 'Our Lady of Mercy Home for Children'. As late as the 1950s and 1960s it was still not easy or acceptable for unmarried mothers to keep their babies.

With changing attitudes in society particularly in the 1970s when the government introduced childcare payments to single mothers, the need for this type of facility was deemed inappropriate. The Mercy Order decided to extend services to entire families in need. The old Foundling Home was demolished in 1979 and a new era of care began.

It is important to note that not all the children admitted to the Waitara Foundling Home were the children of single mothers. The Home/Hospital was initially established for foundlings, as it was felt that while there were institutions for the care of orphans, there were insufficient facilities for foundlings. The high rate of infanticide in the state convinced both Cardinal Moran and the Catholic community that such a facility was urgently required.[290] There were circumstances that made it necessary for children with two parents to be given into the care of the Home. Little Edna Carruthers had both parents living when she died in 1908. William Noud, who died in 1920, also had both parents. And there would have been others not listed here, given into the care of the Mercy Sisters due to family circumstances e.g., sickness or death of the mother or father, desertion or extreme poverty. However the care of foundlings was the main object of establishing the Waitara complex.

WAITARA FOUNDLING HOME - LIST OF BURIALS
Registration No:
    1.   ADAMS, Cecilia Ivy   00773
Born: March 1903, Sydney, NSW

Died: 6 April 1903
Age: 4 weeks old
P.O.D.: Foundling Home, Waitara
Buried: 27 May 1905, R.C. Cemetery, Chatswood

    2.   **BARRY,** James   15364

Born: October 1900, Singleton, NSW
Died: 25 November 1901
P.O.D.: Foundling Home, Waitara
Buried: 26 November 1901, R.C. Cemetery, Chatswood
Medical Attendant: Arthur Grieves
C.O.D.: Teething Convulsions

    3.   **BRADY,** Belinda Marion E.   03338

Born: November 1899, Sydney, NSW
Died: 17 January 1900
Age: 2 months
P.O.D.: Foundling Hospital, Waitara
Buried: 19 January 1900, R.C. Cemetery, Chatswood
Medical Attendant: W. H. O'Neill
C.O.D.: Marasmus

    4.   **BROWN,** Mary   03085

Born: September 1900, Sydney, NSW
Died: 16 December 1900
Age: 3 months
P.O.D.: Foundling Home, Waitara
Buried: 18 December 1900, R. C. Cemetery, Chatswood
Medical Attendant: Walter McD. Kelly
C.O.D.: Marasmus

5. CARRUTHERS, Edna Josephine   15376
Born: July 1908
Died: 2 November 1908
Age: 4 months
P.O.D.: Foundling Home, Waitara
Buried: 5 November 1908, R.C. Cemetery, Chatswood
C.O.D.: Marasmus
Parents: Alfred J. and Vera Carruthers. **N.B.** not an illegitimate child

6. COLLINS, Herbert,   15873
Born: August 1902, Elizabeth Street, Sydney, NSW
Died: 8 December 1902
Age: 3 ½ months old
P.O.D.: Foundling Home, Waitara
Medical Attendant: W.R. Clay, 8 December 1902
C.O.D.: Gastro-Intestinal Catarrh
Religion: not stated
Buried: 11 December 1902, R.C. Cemetery, Chatswood

7. CONNOLLY, Harold   10510
Born: June 1900, Sydney, NSW
Died: 21 July 1900
Age: 6 weeks old
P.O.D.: Foundling Home, Waitara
Medical Attendant: W. McD. Kelly, 17 July 1900
C.O.D.: Gastroenteritis
Buried: 23 July 1900, R.C. Cemetery, Chatswood

8. DOYLE, Reginald   03264
Died: 5 March 1911
Age: 1 year 7 months
P.O.D.: Foundling Home, Waitara, late of St. Margaret's Hospital
Medical Attendant: Sydney C. Watkins

C.O.D.: Tubercular Disease of Bowel
Buried: 6 March 1911, R.C. Cemetery, Chatswood

    9.   **CURRAN, James Walter**   07064

Born: 1902, Sydney, NSW
Died: 15 April 1904
Age: 1 year 9 months
P.O.D.: Foundling Home, Waitara
Medical Attendant: D. Kelly, 13 April 1904
C.O.D.: Pneumonia
Buried: 16 April 1904, R.C. Cemetery, Chatswood

    10.   **CURRAN, Ivy May,**   07088

Born: 1902, Sydney, NSW
Died: 7 May 1904
Age: 1 year 10 months
P.O.D.: Foundling Home, Waitara
Medical Attendant: D. Kelly, 1 May 1904
C.O.D.: Pneumonia, Heart failure
Buried: 11 May 1904, R.C. Cemetery, Chatswood

    11.   **FLYNN, Margaret**   06714

Born: February 1905, Sydney, NSW **Mother:** Rose Flynn
Died: 25 May 1905
Age: 3 months old
P.O.D: Foundling Home, Waitara
C.O.D.: Gastroenteritis
Buried: 27 May 1905, R.C. Cemetery, Chatswood

    12.   **FLYNN, Vincent**   07041

Born: February 1910, Sydney, NSW
Mother: Helen Flynn
Died: 19 April 1910

Age: 2 months old.
P.O.D: Foundling Home, Waitara
C.O.D.: Gastroenteritis
Buried: 22 April 1910, R. C. Cemetery, Chatswood
Remarks: Found at Milsons Point, North Sydney, NSW.

13. HENNESSEY, Alfred John   07022
Born: January 1901, Sydney, NSW
Died: 20 March 1901
Age: 2 months
P.O.D.: Foundling Home, Waitara
Medical Attendant: Walter McD. Kelly
C.O.D.: Marasmus
Buried: 21 March 1901, R.C. Cemetery, Chatswood

14. HOGAN, Paul   02888
Died: 13 January 1905
Age: 3 years 3 months
P.O.D.: Foundling Home, Waitara
Medical Attendant: Walter McD. Kelly
C.O.D.: Pneumonia
Buried: 17 January 1905, R. C. Cemetery, Chatswood

15. KELLY, Frances   11246
Born: May 1901, Sydney, NSW
Died: 16 June 1901
Age: 6 weeks old
P.O.D.: Foundling Home, Waitara
Buried: 17 June 1901, R. C. Cemetery, Chatswood

16. KENNEDY, Edward   15354
Died: 20 November 1901
Age: 5 months

P.O.D.: Foundling Home, Waitara
C.O.D.: Brights Disease, Septicaemia
Buried: 22 November 1901, R.C. Cemetery, Chatswood

17. LYNCH, Robert   03183

Born: December 1903, Newtown, Sydney, NSW
Died: 24 March 1904
Age: 3 months
P.O.D.: Foundling Home, Waitara
Buried: 26 March 1904, R.C. Cemetery, Chatswood.
Medical Attendant: D. Kelly
C.O.D.: Marasmus, Exhaustion

18. McMahon, Mary Veronica   07067

Born: c. 1906, Sydney, NSW
Died: 26 May 1909
Age: 3 years
P.O.D.: Foundling Home, Waitara
Buried: 29 May 1909, R.C. Cemetery, Chatswood

19. McMahon, Monica   07103

Born: c. July, 1903, Sydney
Died: 21 May 1904
Age: 11 months old
P.O.D.: Foundling Home, Waitara
Buried: 23 May 1904, R.C. Cemetery, Chatswood

20. MURPHY, Joseph Richard   06987

Born: March 1900
Died: 28 May 1900
Age: 9 weeks old
P.O.D.: Foundling Home, Waitara
Medical Attendant: W.H. O'Neill, 27 May 1900

C.O.D.: Marasmus
Buried: 29 May 1900, R.C. Cemetery, Chatswood

21. NOLAN, Vincent   03034
Born: November 1900, Sydney, NSW
Died: 15 December 1900
Age: 1 month, at Waitara Foundling Home
Medical Attendant: Walter McD. Kelly
C.O.D.: Marasmus
Buried: 15 December 1900, R.C. Cemetery, Chatswood

22. O'BRIEN, Arthur Milwood   03033
Born: October 1900
Died: 8 December 1900
Age: 2 months old
P.O.D.: Foundling Home, Waitara
Medical Attendant: Walter McD. Kelly, 2 December 1900
C.O.D.: Marasmus
Religion: not stated
Buried: 11 December 1900, R.C. Cemetery, Chatswood

23. O'BRIEN, Thomas Xavier   11157
Born: May 1902, Redfern, NSW
Died: 18 July 1902
Age: 6 weeks old
P.O.D.: Foundling Home, Waitara
Medical Attendant: Arthur Grieves, 16 July 1902
C.O.D.: Gastro Intestinal Catarrh
Buried: 19 July 1902, R.C. Cemetery, Chatswood

24. O'LEARY, Mary Catherine   15848
Born: September 1902, St. Margaret's Hospital, Sydney, NSW
Died: 25 November 1902

P.O.D.: Foundling Home, Waitara
Medical Attendant: Arthur Grieves, 24 November 1902
C.O.D.: Gastro-Intestinal Catarrh
Buried: 26 November 1902, R.C. Cemetery, Chatswood

25. **RILEY, William** 10498

Died: 10 Jul 1900
Age: 4 months
P.O.D.: Foundling Home, Waitara
Medical Attendant: Walter McD. Kelly
C.O.D.: Marasmus
Buried: 12 July 1900, Chatswood

26. **RYAN, Kathleen Winifred** 15365

Born: October 1901, Sydney, NSW **Mother:** Ellen Ryan
Died: 26 November 1901
Age: 6 weeks old
P.O.D.: Foundling Home, Waitara
C.O.D.: Diarrhoea
Buried: 27 November 1901, R.C. Cemetery, Chatswood

27. **RYAN, Stanislaus** 15368

Born: November 1900, Sydney, NSW
Died: 26 November 1901
Age: 1 year old, of Convulsions,
P.O.D.: Foundling Home, Waitara
Buried: 29 November 1901, R. C. Cemetery, Chatswood

28. **RYAN, Teresa** 11231

Born: July 1902, Sydney, NSW
Died: 20 September 1902
Age: 9 weeks old of Gastroenteritis
P. O. D. Foundling Home, Waitara

Buried: 23 September 1902, R. C. Cemetery, Chatswood

29. SULLIVAN, Michael Joseph   15026
Died: 7 December 1909
Age: 2 months
P.O.D.: Foundling Home, Waitara
Medical Attendant: W. R. Clay
C.O.D.: Gastroenteritis
Buried: 9 December 1909, R.C. Cemetery, Chatswood

30. TOOHEY, Frederick,   02751
Born: December 1906, Marrickville, NSW
Died: 24 February 1907, Foundling Home, Waitara, NSW
Medical Attendant: Herbert E. Lee, 23 February 1907
C.O.D.: Chronic Gastroenteritis
Buried: 27 February 1907, R.C. Cemetery, Chatswood

Acknowledgments

Many individuals and history groups have contributed research material to enable this list to be prepared.

My sincere thanks to the following:

Narelle Bartlett, Mrs J.F. Barton, Tewantin, Queensland, Berecry family, Chuter family descendants, Trish Corbett, Max Farley, Gaffey family, Leonie Low, Gillian Kendrigan, A. McCabe, Porter family descendants, Frank Roberts, Ryan family descendants, F. Stephenson, R. Turner, Vos family, Elma Wylie of Adelaide, S.A.

Catholic Parish Chatswood, Christian Brothers Chatswood, Ballarat & District Genealogical Society, Family History Group of Bathurst, Ku-ring-gai Historical Society Inc. (KHS), Manning Valley Historical Society, Goulburn Historical Society, Hornsby Library, Parramatta & District Historical Society, Queanbeyan Family History Centre, Society of Australian Genealogists, Willoughby District Historical Society and Willoughby City Library - Local History section, research companion Robyn Hardie and my family for advice, financial support and patience over many years.

Bibliography

ABBREVIATIONS:
AO: Archives Office
BDM: Births, deaths, marriages
COF: Certificate of Freedom
CP: Catholic Press (newspaper)
FJ: Freemans Journal (newspaper)
GG: Government Gazette
HRA: Historical Records Australia
KHS: Ku-ring-gai Historical Society Inc.
LTO: Land Titles Office
NLA: National Library of Australia
S.A.G.: Society of Australian Genealogists
SMH: Sydney Morning Herald (newspaper)
SRA: NSW State Records Authority, New South Wales
TOL: Ticket of Leave

1 Birth transcript of Esther Cooper born NSW 1891, BDM 32567
2 William Tunks, MLA, letter to Secretary for Lands, 12 March 1867 Edith A. Sims, *Gore Hill Cemetery 1868-1972*

3 Deed of Gift 1863, William Lithgow to Rev. P. Powell, J.S. Ryan, Thos. Cosgrove, LTO, NSW,
 Book 84, No.593

4 H.A. Johnson, S.J. - *A Seed that Grew,* 1956

5 Leplastrier, C., *Willoughby's Fifty Years, A Retrospect, 1865-1915,* Willoughby Municipal Council 1915

6 Death Transcription, NSW Registry BDM, P. A. Alfonso died NSW 1879 No. 03745

7 Death Transcription, NSW Registry BDM, Denis Alfonso, died NSW 1899 No. 07294

8 W. D. Archbold, Ph.D., *The Archbolds of Roseville,* 1997 Seven Star Printing Sydney, p.92

9 Guide to Convict Records *Mary Anne* July 1791, Hannah Murphy, Reel 392, piece 4/4003.SRA/SAG

10 *Sydney Gazette,* 31 July 1819 – R. Archbold, schoolmaster

11 *General Muster List of New South Wales,* 1822, A00378, Archbold, Richard

12 M.R. Sainty, K.A. Johnson, 1980, *1828 Census of NSW,* Library of Australian History, Griffen Press Limited, Archbold, AO 519 – AO 525, p34

13 Catholic Cemetery Chatswood, Local History Section, Willoughby Library, No.7 p.1

14 Historical Records of Australia, HRA 1/X1, 1/XV11, 148, Mitchell Library, Sydney

15 SMH 4 August 1902 Funerals, R. Archbold died at *Clanville,* Roseville.

16 Marriage R. Archbold/M.I.J. Wilson married NSW, 1851, SMH 22 July 1851

17 Early church records, death Sarah Archbold, regn. No. 1534 vol.156

18 Death Transcription, NSW Registry BDM, Catherine Balsom died NSW 1900, No. 10493

19 Marriage Transcription NSW BDM, C. Ryan/L. Balsam married NSW No. 02020

20 Marriage Transcription NSW BDM, M.A. Smith/A. Hodges married NSW 1877 No. 02182

21 Marriage Transcription, NSW BDM, M.J. Smith/J.C. Buhl married NSW 1885 No. 01608

22 Marriage Transcription NSW BDM, E. Smith/J. Gallen married NSW 1884 No. 03330

23 Death Transcription, NSW BDM, Louis Balsam, died NSW 1891 No. 01551

24 Lonely Graves Register, Wattle Flat 1890-1917, Louis Balsam, 4684/1891/No.8 - information supplied by *Family History Group of Bathurst Inc.*

25 NSW Certificate of Naturalisation, Louis Balsamo, 20 March 1877, SA NSW NRS 1041, Roll 130, Register No. 5, p. 81

26 Baptism Transcription, NSW BDM, Richard Beer baptised 1855 No. 328/142

27 Death Transcription NSW BDM, Richard Beer died NSW 1876, No. 04086

28 Immigrant Index 1844-59, Beer family, *Fairlie* 1848/2135/2458- SRA NSW

29 Death Transcription NSW BDM, Margaret Berecry died NSW 1880 No. 00751

30 Death Transcription NSW BDMs, Patrick Berecry/Vercry died NSW 1869, No. 00117

31 Shipping arrival 24 August 1863, Information supplied by descendants of Patrick
 Berecry

32 Death Transcription NSW BDM, Mary C. Borig died NSW 1875 No. 04260

33 NSW Australia Assisted Immigrant Lists, 1828-1896 *Cateaux Wattel,* SRA Reel 2469/1855 M. Borig and family

34 Catholic Cemetery Chatswood, Local History Section, Willoughby Library, No.1, p.1

35 Unassisted Passengers arriving NSW per *Hornet* March 1859, M. Bourke

36 Death of Michael Joseph Bourke, *Freemans Journal,* August 1901

37 Marriage Transcription NSW BDMs, M. Burke (sic)/S.A.E. Porter, NSW 1863 No. 01240

38 Birth Transcription NSW BDM, Bridget Burke, born NSW 1872 No. 5204

39 Death Transcription NSW BDM, Bridget Bourke/Burke died NSW 1885 No. 06431

40 Death Transcription NSW BDM, Ellen Kate Bourke, died NSW 1874, No. 03232

41 Baptism Transcription NSW BDM, Annie M. Boyle, NSW No. 1646/70

42 Death Transcription NSW BDM, Annie M. Boyle, died NSW 1877 No. 01649

43 Death Transcription NSW BDM, Bridget Boyle, died NSW 1867 No. 03498

44 Death Transcription NSW BDM, Catherine Boyle, died NSW 1872 No. 00469

45 Marriage Transcription Early Church Records, NSW BDM, C. O'Brien/Owen Boyle married NSW 1852 No. LO 171/V98

46 Marriage Transcription NSW BDM, Joseph O. Boyle/Emily Thrussell 1886 NSW No. 01132

47 Death Transcription NSW BDM, Owen Boyle died NSW 1891 No. 13728

48 Goulburn Herald *Police Court*, Owen Boyle, Australian Hotel, August 20 1853

49 Goulburn Herald *Insolvency*, Owen Boyle, June 14 1856

50 Goulburn Herald *Robbery of the Rev. Mr Roche,* 26 June 1861.

51 Goulburn Herald, 1853, 1856, 1861, O. Boyle, supplied by Goulburn Historical Society

52 Publicans Licenses ,*Government Gazette* 1853, LIC. No. 0594 issued 26 April 1853.

53 New South Wales Australia Assisted Immigrant Lists 1828-1896 SRA NSW *Pearl* 17 August 1841, www.ancestry.com.au

54 Death Transcription NSW BDM, Philip Boyle died NSW 1873 No. 02777

55 Marriage Transcription NSW BDM, Philip Boyle/Anne Senior, NSW 1870 01473

56 Guide to Convict Records SRA *James Laing* 29 June 1834, Reel 2423 piece 2/8264 p. 65

57 Convict Philip Boyle, *James Laing* TOL 20 November 1838, SRA 931/4/4124

58 Coroner's Court, Death from natural causes, *Empire,* 29 July 1873, p.3

59 Death Transcription NSW BDM, Margaret Brodie died NSW 1865 No. 02190

60 Marriage Transcription NSW BDM, M. Kenn/Kinnear/J. Brodie NSW 1856 BDM 00454

61 Marriage Transcription NSW BDM, P. Gilroy/M.E. Brodie NSW 1879 No. 02139

62 Death Transcription NSW BDM, Edward Brophy died NSW 1871, No. 02461

63 Baptism Transcription Early Church Records NSW BDMS Henry Brophy NSW 1837/1289/126

64 Convict Indent no. 158 *Royal Admiral,* (5) 1835/prisoner no. 35/409

65 TOL, Edward Brophy No. 42/2270, 28 September 1842, SR NSW Reel 945

66 Death Transcription NSW BDM, Margaret Brophy died NSW 1886 No. 06092

67 Death Transcription NSW BDM, Catherine Burke died NSW 1873 No. 02749

68 Death Transcription NSW BDM, Sarah Ann Burke died NSW 1895 No. 10697

69 Mollie Gillen, *The Founders of Australia, A biographical dictionary of the First Fleet,* p.23

70 Gillen, Ibid, Randall/Reynolds John (c. 1764) p. 298

71 Death Transcription NSW BDM, Walter Burke died NSW 1879 No. 03704

72 Death Transcription NSW BDM, William Burke, died NSW 1890 No. 12110

73 Information supplied by Parramatta & District Historical Society – W. Burke

74 Death Transcription NSW BDM, Ann M. Callen died NSW 1898 No. 11330

75 Marriage Transcription Ann Matthew/J. Callen NSW 1847 No. 744/131

76 Index of Assisted passengers arriving NSW 1841, *Fairlie,* Reel 2134/piece 4/4788 p. 286

77 Death Transcription NSW BDM, John Callen died NSW 1898 No.10855

78 Convict indent, John Callen per *Waverley*, 17 June 1839, 4/4404 reel 1022 C.O.F. 46/530 4/4180 Reel 950 SRA NSW - Information supplied by J.F. Barton, Queensland

79 Death Transcription NSW BDM, Ann Cherry died NSW 1879 No. 03725

80 Catholic Cemetery Chatswood, Local History Section, Willoughby Library, No. 44 p.5

81 Death Transcription NSW BDM, John Cherry died NSW 1881 No. 04328

82 Marriage Transcription NSW BDM, A. Marsh/J. Cherry NSW 1880 No. 00674

83 Probate No. 5493 Series 3, Reel 4064 6/7825, SRA NSW

84 SMH 4 March 1881 – Report of Inquest into death of John Cherry.

85 Death Transcription NSW BDM, Catherine Chuter died NSW 1871 No. 02439

86 Marriage Transcription NSW BDM, W. Chuter/C. Ryan NSW 1861 No. 01084

87 Marriage Transcription NSW BDM, William Chuter/Susannah Lavender NSW 1851/NU V 245/37B

88 Catholic Cemetery Chatswood, loc. cit. No. 41 C. Chuter

89 Marriage Transcription NSW BDM, C. Ryan/T. Robertson NSW 1861 No. 00774

90 Marriage Transcription NSW BDM, William Chuter/C. Robertson NSW 1875 No.00392

91 Death Transcription NSW BDM Thomas Robertson died NSW 1869 No. 02436

92 St. Mary's North Sydney Baptism Register William Chuter baptised 1876

93 Death Transcription NSW BDM William Chuter died NSW 1882 No. 04959

94 Government Gazette 1867, p.3002 application to purchase land at Berry's Bay No.40 of section 8 of Chuter Estate

95 Death Transcription NSW BDM Catherine Collins, NSW 1872 No. 02696

96 SMH October 1852, Family notices J & J Collins

97 Death Transcription NSW BDM Francis Collins died NSW 1886 No. 06122

98 Assisted passengers colony NSW January 1841, *Spitfire SRA NSW f Collins*

99 Death Transcription NSW BDM John Collins, died NSW 1881 No.04276

100 SMH 23 May 1881, John Collins, Family Notices

101 Catholic Cemetery Chatswood, Local History Section, Willoughby Library, No. 20 p.3.

102 Birth Transcription Early Church Records NSW BDM, J. J. Connor, No. 1851/1941/141

103 Death Transcription NSW BDM J.J. Connor died NSW 1882 No. 04986

104 Marriage Transcription NSW BDM, James Connor/C. Gallagher, NSW 1870 No. 0147

105 Death Transcription NSW BDM, Julia Connor died NSW 1870 No. 02250

106 Index to Miscellaneous immigrants, arriving in colony of NSW October 1836 per *Duchess of Northumberland,* SR NSW. Information supplied by Leonie Low, descendant

107 Death Transcription, NSW BDM Michael Connor died NSW 1884 No. 05858

108 Marriage Register St. Mary's Cathedral M. Connor/J. Quilligan V 1837 279 V 90, microfiche SAG

109 Convict No. 29/351 *Sophia*, 17 Jan 1829. Film 398 Shelf 4/4014 p. 013 SRA NSW -

110. TOL M. Connor issued 3 June 1837, No. SRA NSW reel 927/37/913

111 Death Transcription NSW BDM E.A. Connolly NSW 1878 No. 03885

112 Death Transcription NSW BDM John Connolly NSW 1882 No. 04869

113 Marriage Transcription, Early Church Records, held at NSW Registry BDMs, John Connolly/M. Collins NSW 1854 No. 514 V 100

114 Death Rebecca Connolly, died NSW 1854 LA V1854/396/143, Microfiche, SAG

115 Death Transcription NSW BDM Mary A. Connolly, died NSW 1884 No. 05863

116 Death Transcription NSW BDM William M. Connolly died NSW 1885 No. 06368

117 Death Transcription NSW BDM Ada M. Cooke, died NSW 1872 No. 02707

118 Marriage Transcription NSW BDM J.H. Cook/M. Elliss NSW 1862, No. 01114

119 Death Transcription NSW BDM A. Cosgrove died NSW 1868 No. 02498

120 Death Transcription NSW BDM Thomas Cosgrove died NSW 1871 No. 002470

121 Marriage Transcription NSW BDM T. Cosgrove/E. Berkelman NSW 1854 No.449/100

122 Probate. No. 9869 Series 1 Reel 4053 SRA NSW T. Cosgrove

123 Death Transcription NSW BDM Timothy Cusick died NSW 1893 No. 13463

124 Probate No. 6587 Series 4 Letters of Administration SRA NSW T. Cusick

125 Cusick family, information supplied by Tasmanian Family History Society

126 Death Transcription NSW BDM Bernard Daly died NSW 1877 No. 03322

127 Marriage Transcription Early Church Records, B. Daly/ I. Beirne NSW V1853 568/99 LD held at NSW Registry BDMs

128 Marriage Transcription B. Daly/C. Collins NSW Registry BDM 1856 No. 00956

129 NSW Australia Assisted Immigrant Lists 1828-1896 B. Daly 16 August 1841 SRA. www.ancestry.com.au

130 SMH 9 October1876 Catherine Daly Death Notice - registration not found

131 Death Transcription NSW BDM M. E. Daly died NSW 1883 No. 04874

132 Death Transcription NSW BDM J. F. Daly died NSW 1890 No. 11962

133 Birth Transcription NSW BDM Timothy Dennehy born NSW 1900 No. 07267

134 Death Transcription NSW BMS Timothy. Dennehy died NSW 1904, No. 03134

135 Death Transcription NSW BDM John Donnolly died NSW 1880 No. 04207

136 Death Transcription NSW BDM John W. Donnolly/Donelly, NSW 1869 No. 02423

137 Death Transcription NSW BDM William Donnolly, died NSW 1865, No. 02212

138 Marriage Transcription Early Church Records, NSW BDM William Donnolly/M. Kelly NSW 1840 574 V90

139 William Donnelly/Donnolly, *Bells Life in Sydney & Sporting Review,* 4 April 1846

140 Water Police Court, *Empire* 14 January 1865, p. 2, William Donnelly

141 Supreme Court of NSW Probate No.6666, Series 1, SRA NSW Reel 4049/6/7801

142 Death Transcription NSW BDM Johann Ebert died NSW 1870 No. 02280

143 Passengers arriving from Germany *Cateaux Wattel* 1855 SRA Reel 2469

144 Water Police Court, John Ebert v John Fennessey, *Empire,* 16 March, 1867 p.8 nla trove article 60837640

145 Death Transcription NSW BDM, Christopher J. Emmett died NSW 1899 No. 01190

146 Marriage Transcription NSW BDM C.J. Emmett/J.A. Frost NSW 1891 No. 07281

147 Death Transcription NSW BDM, John Fennessy died NSW 1868 No. 02500

148 Marriage Transcription NSW BDM, J. Fennessy/C. Lyons NSW 1859 No. 01159

149 Birth Transcription NSW BDM, John Flynn born NSW 1866 No. 00969

150 SMH Death Notice John Flynn died NSW 12 July 1889

151 Death Transcription NSW BDM, Margaret Flynn died NSW 1889 No. 01159

152 Marriage certificate M. Reynolds/Patrick Flynn NSW 1865 BDM 00367

153 Death Transcription Patrick G. Flynn died NSW 1891 No. 01975

154 Death Transcription NSW BDM, Catherine Ford died NSW 1894 No. 12594

155 Death Transcription NSW BDM, Elsie Gaffey died NSW 1902 No. 03006

156 Death Transcription NSW BDM, Johanna Glover died NSW 1871 No. 02453

157 Marriage Transcription NSW Registry H.H. Glover/J. Farrell NSW 1856 BDM No. 02646

158 Death Transcription NSW BDM, Henry H. Glover died NSW 1904 No. 07123

159 Death Transcription NSW BDM, Sydney H. Glover died NSW 1871 No. 02454

160 Death Transcription NSW Registry, Charles Golding died NSW 1879 BDM No. 03733

161 Certificate of Freedom Convict No.40/1840, C. Goulding March 1850 No. 50/174

162 Death Transcription NSW BDM, Elizabeth Goulding died NSW 1907, No. 11193

163 Baptism Transcription Early Church Records, Edward Cullen born NSW 1844 No. 1646 V63, held at NSW Registry BDMs

164 Convict 2248 Elizabeth Hill per *Mary Anne,* Port Philip, April 1839.. Information supplied by Queanbeyan Family History Society

165 Supreme Court of NSW Probate Index Vol. G 1902-1910 No.17 E. Goulding, No. 40681 State Library NSW

166 Death Transcription Mary K. Guinane died NSW 1904 BDM No. 14745

167 Death Transcription Margaret Harnett died NSW 1868 Registry BDM No. 02497

168 Harnett family information supplied by Willoughby District Historical Society
169 Death Transcription NSW BDM, William Harvey died NSW 1909 No. 11069
170 Death Transcription NSW BDM, Lawrence Howard died NSW 1905 No. 08472
171 NSW Australia Assisted Immigrant Lists 1828-1896 per *Alfred* 1860 SRA NSW
172 Death Transcription, Mary Howard died NSW 1908 BDM No. 01066
173 Immigrants arriving NSW (1846 – 1859) Mary Howard, Reel 2136/2464 SRA NSW
174 Death Transcription NSW BDM, Louisa I. Jarvis died NSW 1901 BDM No. 12167
175 Chatswood Catholic Cemetery op. cit. No. 48 p. 6. C. Lofberg
176 St. Mary's North Sydney Baptism register Clara Lofberg, baptised December 1878
177 Death Transcription NSW Registry, Jonas Lofberg died NSW 1880 BDM No. 01596
178 Naturalisation certificate Jonas Lofberg Register No. 3 page 99 1869 SRA NSW
179 Probate No. 6159 Series 3 Reel 4065 6/7826 SRA NSW J. Lofberg
180 Information death George B Lofberg 1872 supplied by Ku ring gai Family History Society
181 Death Transcription NSW Registry, Andrew J. Lynch died NSW 1882, BDM 00272
182 Death Transcription NSW Registry BDM, Andrew M. Lynch died NSW 1890 No. 00120

183 Death Transcription NSW, Hannah T. Lynch died NSW 1884 BDM No. 02082

184 Death Transcription NSW Registry, Margaret McGlinchy died NSW 1897 BDM 10655

185 Death Transcription Mary McKay died NSW 1877 BDM No. 00337

186 SMH (Jo) Hannah McKell, death notices 20 April 1901

187 Marriage Transcription Hannah Ryan/John Mackell NSW 1865 BDM No. 00722

188 Death Transcription Mary T. MacKell died NSW 1884 BDM No. 05861

189 Death Transcription, Ellen McMahon died NSW 1899 BDM 03266

190 Thorne, L.G., *North Shore Sydney from 1788 to Today*, Sydney 1968, pp 62-64

191 Saddington, M., Thomas Boyd, Toulouse Farm, *The Historian* Volume 3, No. 4, KHS

192 Death Transcription NSW Registry BDM, Thomas Boyd died NSW 1858 No. 02379

193 Census of 1828, M. R. Sainty and K.A. Johnson 1980, op. cit. p254

194 Death Transcription Owen McMahon died NSW 1885 BDM No. 06452

195 *Jess's Girls Female Convicts* 1788-1818 Ann Byrne/Burne SAG Reel 4006

196 *Marsden's Female Muster, 1806,* Ann Burne per *Rolla* CO 162, S.A.G.

197 Death Transcription Thomas McMahon died NSW 1875 BDM No. 04282

198 Death Transcription NSW BDM, William O. McMahon died NSW 1899 No. 03450

199 Marriage Transcription William O. McMahon/Hannah Redgrave, 1861, BDM 01090

200 SMH 8 March 1899, Death notices William O. McMahon

201 Information supplied by Manning River Valley Family History Society

202 Death Transcription NSW Registry Cornelius Maloney died NSW 1888 BDM 06140

203 Water Police Court, D. Ryan and Cornelius Maloney, *Empire* 28 March 1867

204 Death Transcription Ellen Maloney died NSW 1896 BDM 11580

205 Chatswood Catholic Cemetery List, John Maloney, No. 18 p. 2

206 Death Transcription James C.C. Mathew died NSW 1868, BDM No. 02517

207 Mathew family information supplied by J.F. Barton, Queensland.

208 Death Transcription Peter Mulloney died NSW 1872 BDM No. 02711

209 Death Transcription John Murphy died NSW 1880 BDM No. 04823

210 Death Transcription Rev. John P. O'Flynn died NSW 1881 BDM No. 04240

211 Death Transcription NSW Registry Margaret O'Grady died NSW 1892 BDM 12216

212 Probate No. 3653 Series 4, SRA NSW Reel 4087 6/7869 M. O'Grady

213 Death Transcription William O'Grady died NSW 1887 BDM 05429

214 Marriage Transcription William. O' Grady/ M. Reynolds NSW 1882 BDM 03047

215 Death Transcription NSW Registry Mary Oliver died NSW 1879 BDM 03703

216 Charles Swancott *Dee Why to Barrenjoey and Pitt Water* c. 1970 page 28

217 Death Transcription Frances Parfitt died NSW 1891 BDM 13785

218 Parfitt Family information supplied by Parramatta & District Historical Society

219 Death Transcription John Pendergast/Prendergast died NSW 1885 BDM 08991

220 Evening News (Sydney NSW) 5 January 1885 Coroner's Report of Inquest into death

221 John Pendergast, SMH Wed. 18 March 1885, p.4. Not guilty verdict Thomas Foster

222 Immigrants arriving NSW per *La Hogue* 21 October 1878, Reel 2141 SRA

223 Death Transcription Clara T. Porter died NSW 1909 BDM 11089

224 Death Transcription Ernest F. Porter died NSW 1898 BDM 11366

225 Death Transcription Ernest Reginald died NSW 1895 BDM 10689

226 Death Transcription John A. Porter died NSW 1879 BDM 03662

227 Death Transcription John A. Porter died NSW 1908 BDM 07191

228 Death Transcription John J. Porter died NSW 1901 BDM 11306

229 Death Transcription Sarah A. Porter died NSW 1891 BDM 05879

230 Marriage Transcription S.A. McMahon/William Porter NSW 1869 BDM 00167

231 William J. Porter, died NSW 1901 BDM 0065

232 Michael Flynn, *The Second Fleet 1790, Surprise* p 482 Richard Porter

233 Guide to Convict Records AONSW *Surprise* Second Fleet, 1790 Reel 2662 4/4003 A S.A.G.

234 Convicts per *Mary Anne* July, 1791 Reel 392 4/4003 SRA

235 Gay Halstead *The Story of St Ives (NSW)* – The Porter family p. 125

236 Death Transcription Michael J. Power, died NSW 1880 BDM No. 00814

237 Marriage Transcription M. J. Power/M. Walsh NSW 1864 BDM 01284

238 Death Transcription Matilda A. Power died NSW 1874 BDM 03207

239 Birth Transcription Henrietta E. Radke born NSW 1865 BDM No. 04492

240 Chatswood Catholic Cemetery List, No. 36 p.4, H. Radke

241 Chatswood Catholic Cemetery List, No. 35 p.4, Francis Reynolds

242 Catholic Cemetery Chatswood loc. cit. Honorah/Norah Reynolds

243 Death Transcription Norah Reynolds died NSW 1871 BDM 02413

244 Catholic Cemetery Chatswood, loc. cit. No. 33 p.4, James Reynolds

245 Marriage Transcription James Reynolds/Elizabeth Wade NSW 1901 BDM 02885

246 Catholic Cemetery Chatswood op.cit.No.57 p.6, M. Reynolds

247 Catholic Cemetery Chatswood, loc. cit. No.56, P. Reynolds

248 Information supplied by Ku-ring-gai Historical Society and Ballarat & District Genealogical Society

249 Death Transcription NSW Registry John Riley died NSW 1873, BDM No. 02748

250 Death Transcription Margaret Riley died NSW 1871 BDM No. 02465

251 Death Transcription Eveline S. Roberts died NSW 1880 BDM 04792

252 Death Transcription John R. Roberts died NSW 1877 BDM 03328

253 Death Transcription Annie Matilda Robinson died NSW 1908 BDM 05048

254 Marriage Transcription Joseph Robinson/A. M. McIntosh NSW 1899 BDM 03360

255 Death Transcription James J. Roche died NSW 1904 BDM No. 13706

256 Death Transcription Mathew Ryan died NSW 1879 BDM No. 03695

257 Shipping details supplied by Ryan family descendants

258 Death Certificate supplied by Ryan family descendants, Winifred Ryan died 1889

259 Catholic Cemetery Chatswood loc. cit. No. 54 p.6

260 Death Transcription Frank Scully died NSW 1897 BDM 13528

261 Death Transcription Mary Slattery died NSW 1897 BDM 10666

262 Marriage Transcription M. Reynolds/William Slattery NSW BDM 03740

263 Death Transcription William Slattery died NSW 1889 BDM 02047

264 Birth Transcription William Patrick Slattery born NSW 1887 BDM 02951

265 Catholic Cemetery Chatswood, op. cit. No. 53 p. 6

266 Marriage Transcription Charles J. Swanson/Ellen Collins, NSW 1869 BDM 01544

267 Death certificate William J. Tweedy died NSW 1908 BDM 07262 supplied N. Roberts

268 TOL 40/957 Convict William J. Tweedy granted November 1849

269 Certificates and details of William J. Tweedy's marriage, land purchases, will and funeral supplied by Narelle Bartlett

270 Death Transcription Martinus J. Vos died NSW 1910 BDM 13014

271 Marriage Transcription M. Vos/Margaret Pammenter NSW 1898 BDM 08477

272 Marriage Transcription Margaret Vos/J.P. Mason NSW 1913 BDM 06088

273 Death Transcription NSW Registry John White died NSW 1882 BDM 04850

274 Death Transcription Emily Wiles died NSW 1875 BDM 04312

275 Passengers arriving 1855-1922; Shipping Master's Office; L. Wiles Master *Australian* from South Seas to Sydney, 23 January 1854, Mrs Wiles and child, SRA NSW NRS 13278 reel 399

276 Passengers arriving 1826-1859, *Australian* Lewin Wiles Master, from a Whaling Voyage to Port Jackson, 12 May 1852, Mrs Wiles passenger and son. SRA NSW reel 1279

277 Death Transcription William Willoughby died NSW 1881 BDM 04301

278 English Census 1861, Bolton, Lancashire, William Willoughby and family, www.ancestry.com.au
279 Supreme Court of NSW Probate No. 6121 Series 3, William Willoughby died 2 September 1881, SRA reel 4065/6/7826
280 English Census 1871, Windsor, William Willoughby and family, www.ancestry.com.au
281 SMH 10 February 1891 Benevolent Asylum Committee Meeting
282 SMH 8 October 1890 Benevolent Asylum Board Meeting
283 Australian Town & Country Journal 3 December 1892, P.45 Discoveries of Dead Infants
284 The Bathurst Post (NSW 1881-1922), 15 May 1894, p.7 Baby Farming
285 Catholic Press 28 July 1900, p.17 The Foundling Home Waitara
286 Evening News (Sydney) 17 March 1899, p.4 Abandoned Infant, Milson's Point Line
287 CP Saturday 6 May 1899 pp.2, 3. An Afternoon at Waitara
288 Evening News 27 April 1900 p.3. Left in a Waiting Room
289 Vincent Flynn, Waitara Foundling Home, List of Burials, No. 12 BDM 07041
290 CP Saturday 6 May 1899, pp 2,3. An Afternoon at Waitara

Notes

Notes

Notes

Notes

Notes

www.ingramcontent.com/pod-product-compliance
Lightning Source LLC
Chambersburg PA
CBHW031122080526
44587CB00011B/1069